Relish

NORTH EAST & YORKSHIRE

SECOND HELPING

Original recipes from the North East and
Yorkshire's finest chefs and restaurants.
Introduction by Kenny Atkinson.

First Published 2015
By Relish Publications
Shield Green Farm, Tritlington,
Northumberland, NE61 3DX.

Twitter: @Relish_Cookbook
Facebook: RelishRestaurantGuide
For cookbooks and recipes visit:
www.relishpublications.co.uk
For publishing enquiries visit:
www.relish-publishing.co.uk

ISBN: 978-0-9934678-0-6

Publisher: Duncan L Peters
General Manager: Teresa Peters
Design: Vicki Brown
Relish Photography: Tim Green, Kevin Gibson,
Nicky Rogerson
Editorial Consultant: Paul Robertson
Twitter: @paulrobbo1966
Proofing Coordinator: Valerie McLeod
Sales: Wendy Rutterford
Coordinator: Rebecca Laycock

Front cover photograph by: Nicky Rogerson

Printed in Poland on behalf of Latitude Press

Relish
PUBLICATIONS

OUR HAND PICKED RESTAURANTS

As the proud owner of a Relish cookbook, you may subscribe for your own personal Relish Rewards card which entitles you to free membership for one year.

You can access the Relish members' area on our website and find out what exclusive offers are available to you from the fantastic restaurants featured in our series of books throughout the UK.

SUBSCRIBE FOR YOUR REWARD CARD ON OUR HOMEPAGE
Simply register your name, address and title of Relish book purchased to receive your **FREE Relish Reward Card**
www.relishpublications.co.uk

When you make a reservation, simply let the restaurant know that you are a member and take your card along with you.

WHAT ARE THE REWARDS?
The rewards will continue to be updated on the website so do check and keep in touch. These range from a free bottle of Champagne to free gifts when you dine. Relish will send you a quarterly newsletter with special discounts, rewards and free recipes. We are about quality not quantity!

All offers are subject to change. See the Relish website for details.

www.relishpublications.co.uk

004
CONTENTS

006
CONTENTS

009
STARTERS

011
MAINS

013
DESSERTS

015

FOREWORD BY KENNY ATKINSON

Whether it is the bustle of our city centres, the beauty of our coast or the tranquillity of our countryside - the North East and Yorkshire boasts many attractions in stunning surroundings.

With so many quality dining venues popping up across both regions, they are also starting to be recognised for its fantastic food offering too.

For me, the North East and Yorkshire is home to some of the best produce in the UK and I've enjoyed demonstrating the regions' rich pickings through my achievements, both at the restaurant and through my success on BBC2's hit TV show, Great British Menu.

As a Newcastle-based chef, I feel very proud to have access to such high quality produce and I am privileged to have the opportunity to share it with diners at House of Tides. Something we endeavour to promote at the restaurant is the importance of provenance and food sustainability, which is why we source as much produce as possible from the local area.

Over the past year or so we have seen a great many cafés, gastropubs and restaurants opening up across the area, offering a diverse range of cuisine to suit all tastes and budgets, it's clear to see that the local dining scene is headed for exciting times.

Even though the economic problems of the last few years have thrown up great challenges for businesses and their customers, not to mention the terrible weather that producers have had to contend with, the North East and Yorkshire has, in my opinion, not only won the battle but emerged even stronger as a result.

We are all passionate about and proud of our area, our food and our service. I am delighted to give you a taste of what we all have to offer through the pages of this superb book.

So, all that remains is to wish those working in the North East and Yorkshire's amazing food and drink scene another successful year and to encourage food lovers in the area to make the most of the fantastic array of produce - and restaurants - available on their doorstep.

Kenny Atkinson, House of Tides

016
HOME COMFORTS

Rolling countryside, golden beaches, National Parks, heritage sites of international significance, friendly people and a wonderful larder of varied local produce brought to life by talented chefs.

Passionate people, passionate places and a welcome like no other is our trademark.

Yet the North East and Yorkshire regions have for so long been underrated by foodies outside our borders but, as the pages of our second helping show, the burgeoning talent can no longer be ignored.

Those of us born and bred here need no convincing - we know only too well how the culinary offering has gone from strength to strength with more award winners than ever plating up glorious dishes for regulars and visitors alike.

The kitchen was at the heart of family life during the post war industrial era when the landscape was dominated by mining, factories and shipyards.

Good, wholesome food was the fuel which fired the men and women working long shifts in difficult conditions to power the economy and families. Just the smell of cooking and baking evokes powerful memories of my own childhood within a mining community, while home cooking was the inspiration for so many of our chefs.

Much of the heavy industry may have gone but the passion for food remains strong with the tradition of making the most of the fruits of the land and sea, forged on the fish quays and in many an allotment, providing the back story for what we have today.

Too often when politicians talk of the Northern Powerhouse the imaginary line seems to be drawn at Manchester when there is so much to offer in the counties leading up to the Scottish Borders.

The Tour de France and Tour of Britain cycle races were just two events which helped showcase the Yorkshire and North East regions - a key factor in driving not only more staycation visitors to sample their delights but also tempting an increasing number of international tourists here through our ports and airports.

Being so close to and in some cases actually on the coast, our restaurateurs have access to the freshest possible fish and seafood. Our green and pleasant land offers unrivalled grazing, providing the perfect environment to rear the best quality meat for our plates.

The forests are an adventure playground for foragers while our passion for growing award-winning vegetables is still in evidence.

So, whether it is discovering exciting new foods or the best classical cooking in the country, the North East and Yorkshire is the place to be. It is surely only a matter of time before we see more Michelin stars, AA Rosettes and entries into the Good Food Guide.

This book takes you to some restaurants who have already achieved these accolades or are well on their way - each with menus to get your gastric juices flowing.

They need your support so make sure you sample as many of them as you can. Once you have done that, then you can experience your favourite dishes again by recreating them in your own kitchen thanks to the recipes generously donated by our chefs.

There really is no place like home.

Paul Robertson, Editor. Twitter: @paulrobbo1966

018
ARTISAN

The Biscuit Factory, Stoddart Street, Newcastle upon Tyne, NE2 1AN

0191 260 5411
www.artisannewcastle.com Twitter: @artisan_NE

Situated in The Biscuit Factory, the UK's largest arts, craft and design gallery, artisan is influenced by its location in Newcastle's cultural quarter, with creative flourishes of originality in the furnishings and an impressive 25 foot glass wall showcasing the latest collections of contemporary sculpture on display in the adjoining gallery.

Spacious and modern in its design, yet intimate and informal in its feel, artisan is a place to luxuriate in great surroundings with great food.

Sourcing from the fields, the foragers and the fishermen, the British inspired menus use the finest regional and seasonal ingredients. The kitchen is headed up by North East Chef of the Year winner, Andrew Wilkinson and he is inspired by daily hauls from local producers and suppliers to create menus which balance a delicacy of technique with an intensity of fresh flavour.

Artisan offers an unparalleled culinary experience with artistically designed dining spaces for private use by guests and they can even arrange private access to their beautiful gallery.

Regularly ranked among the top 10 restaurants in the city on Trip Advisor, artisan has also received national recognition, having been listed as one of the top 25 restaurants in the UK for Sunday lunch by The Times newspaper. The restaurant is also one of only a handful in Tyne and Wear to feature in the Good Food Guide 2016.

Artisan's award-winning chef uses creativity and flair to craft classic dishes with a twist; offering diners a unique and truly memorable dining experience.

WILD WATERCRESS PANNA COTTA WITH SMOKED EEL, BEETROOT & HORSERADISH

SERVES 4

Verdejo, Sauvignon Blanc, Viña Garedo (Spain)
A zesty and acidic wine that cuts through the smoky
eel but complements the flavour of the beetroot.

Ingredients

100g smoked eel

Wild Watercress Panna Cotta

300ml full-fat milk
100ml double cream
2 leaves gelatine (soaked)
50g wild watercress
salt and pepper

Beetroot

heritage baby beetroots (selection of)
1 clove garlic (crushed)
olive oil (drizzle of)

Dressing

1 tsp Dijon mustard
white wine vinegar (splash of)
100ml olive oil
salt and pepper

Sourdough Croutons

sourdough loaf (small)
clarified butter

Garnish

wild watercress
wild flowers
fresh horseradish

4 dariole moulds (chilled)

Method

For The Wild Watercress Panna Cotta (Prepare the day before)

Bring the milk and cream gently to the boil. Squeeze the
gelatine leaves dry and add to the pan, together with the
watercress. Transfer the mix to a liquidiser, season with salt and
pepper, then blend for approximately 30 seconds until it is a
vibrant green colour. Pass through a *chinois* and pour the
mixture into the moulds leaving a few millimetres at the top.
Set in the fridge overnight.

Chef's Tip

Liquidise the ingredients for the panna cotta as soon as
possible and chill for freshness.

For The Beetroot

Preheat the oven to 180°C (fan).

Wash the beetroot and wrap in tin foil with the garlic and olive
oil. Place in the oven for 20 minutes. Allow to cool for 5 minutes,
then pop them out of their skins.

For The Dressing

Add the mustard, white wine vinegar and olive oil to a bowl
and season with salt and pepper. Stir until combined and use
the dressing to marinate the warm beetroots.

For The Sourdough Croutons

Preheat the oven to 160°C (fan).

Thinly slice the sourdough loaf and brush the slices with *clarified
butter*. Place on a baking tray in the oven for 8 minutes.

For The Smoked Eel

Check for bones and cut into bite-sized pieces.

For The Garnish

Pick a selection of flowers and wild watercress and wash in
cold water.

To Assemble The Dish

Remove the panna cottas from the moulds and place on the
plates with a few pieces of eel and beetroot on the side.
Carefully position the croutons and garnishes on the plate.
Grate fresh horseradish over the dish.

RUMP & GLAZED BELLY OF LAMB WITH BRAISED LETTUCE, PEAS & GIROLLES

SERVES 4

🍷 *Quinta de Chocapalha, Tinto (Portugal)*
A heavy wine to cope with the richness of the lamb, yet light enough to complement the creamy gratin potatoes.

Ingredients

Lamb Belly And Lamb Sauce
2 lamb bellies (boned and rolled, seasoned)
1 carrot (diced), 1 onion (diced)
1 stick celery (diced)
1 bay leaf, 1 sprig thyme
2 white peppercorns (crushed)
4 fresh tomatoes (chopped)
200ml white wine, 800ml chicken stock

Lamb Rump
4 x 250g lamb rumps
1 tbsp oil, 1 sprig thyme
butter paper
1 clove garlic, 1 sprig rosemary
oil and butter (to cook)

Gratin Dauphinoise Potatoes
8 Albert Bartlett potatoes (washed, peeled)
500ml double cream
4 peppercorns
1 bay leaf, 1 sprig thyme
5 cloves garlic (thinly sliced)
salt and pepper

Pea Purée
500g fresh peas
unsalted butter (knob of)
salt and pepper (to season)

Vegetables
4 baby grelot onions (halved lengthways)
2 baby gem lettuces (outer leaves removed)
1 tbsp water, 200g girolle mushrooms
peas (handful of, *blanched*)
1 sprig thyme, butter (knob of)

Chef's Tip
The lamb should be warm, not piping hot, when served.

Method

For The Lamb Belly And Sauce

Preheat the oven to 130°C (fan).

Seal the belly in a hot pan with oil for 10 minutes, then remove from the pan. Add the diced vegetables and sauté for 5-10 minutes. Add the bay leaf, peppercorns and thyme. Stir in the tomatoes, then pour in the wine and reduce. Return the belly to the pan with the chicken stock and any spare lamb bones. Simmer, skim the fat off the top and cook in the oven for 2½ hours. Cut the belly into slices and add to the pan with the lamb sauce. Bring the pan to a simmer and transfer to the oven for 6-7 minutes. Keep basting to ensure the lamb belly is sticky and glazed.

For The Lamb Rump

Marinate the lamb rump with the oil, thyme, garlic and rosemary for 30 minutes or ideally, overnight.

Preheat the oven to 190°C (fan).

Lightly score the rumps, remove any sinew and keep the skin on. Cook with a touch of lamb fat or vegetable oil, skin-side down, until caramelised. Add butter paper to the pan and place the lamb skin-side down, then cook in the oven for 8-9 minutes. Add a knob of butter, rosemary, thyme and garlic to the pan and baste the lamb. Leave to rest for 12 minutes on a wire rack.

For The Gratin Dauphinoise Potatoes

Preheat the oven to 150°C (fan).

Thinly slice the potatoes (2-3 mm). Add the double cream to a pan with the peppercorns, bay leaf, thyme and garlic. Simmer to infuse for 10 minutes. Layer the potatoes with the cream, adding salt and pepper, in an ovenproof dish. Place in a *bain-marie* and cook in the oven for 45 minutes until you can easily pierce with a knife.

For The Pea Purée

Cook the peas in a little salted, boiling water until tender. Transfer to a liquidiser with the butter to create a shiny, velvety texture. Season with salt and pepper and pass through a *chinois*.

For The Vegetables

Place the onions cut-side down in the pan with butter. Place the baby gem to the same pan. Add a tablespoon of water and thyme, cook for 8 minutes. Remove the onions and lettuce, add the girolles to the pan along with fresh, *blanched* peas.

To Assemble The Dish

Add a dollop of the pea purée, then place the belly on the plate surrounded by the vegetables. Finish with a thickly cut slice of the rump on top and a generous serving of lamb sauce. Serve the gratin dauphinoise potatoes in a separate dish.

ICED RASPBERRY PARFAIT, SUMMER FRUITS & LEMON MERINGUE

SERVES 8

Rose Spumante Brut 'Le Colture' NV (Italy)
With undertones of strawberry, this wine perfectly complements the summer fruits in this dish, but is sharp enough to cope with the pungent lemon curd and yoghurt.

Ingredients

Iced Raspberry Parfait
285ml double cream
1 egg white, 3 egg yolks
2 tbsp water, 125g caster sugar
50g raspberry purée (or to taste)

Lemon Curd
3 lemons (juice and zest of)
200g caster sugar
200g butter, 4 egg yolks

Yoghurt Sorbet
400g fresh full-fat natural yoghurt
200ml water, 200g caster sugar
½ lemon (juice of)

Raspberry Tuile
21g Demerara sugar, 21g caster sugar
18g plain flour
21g raspberry purée, 21g butter (melted)
½g red food colouring

Italian Meringue
180g caster sugar
100ml water, 3 egg whites
1 drop lemon juice

Candied Fennel
1 bulb fennel, 150g sugar, 150ml water

Sable Biscuit
400g butter (soft)
200g icing sugar (sifted), 500g plain flour
2 egg yolks, salt (pinch of)

Summer Fruits
I small punnet strawberries
1 punnet raspberries
oxalis or wild wood sorrel
apple marigold leaves

Method

For The Iced Raspberry Parfait (Prepare the day before)

Whisk the cream until it's almost forming stiff peaks. Whisk the egg white until firm. Whisk the yolks until pale. Boil the water and sugar in a pan to 120°C, then pour this onto the egg yolks while beating. Continue to beat until cool. Fold in the raspberry purée, followed by the cream and egg whites. Freeze overnight.

For The Lemon Curd

Add all the ingredients, except the egg yolks, into a *bain-marie* and melt slowly. Stir in the yolks and whisk for 10 minutes until thick. Pass through a *chinois*.

For The Yoghurt Sorbet

Simmer the water and sugar in a pan and boil for 5 minutes until slightly thickened. Allow to cool, then add in the yoghurt and lemon to taste. Churn in an ice cream machine.

For The Raspberry Tuile

Mix together all the dry ingredients. Add the raspberry purée, melted butter and food colouring, then spread evenly on a baking tray. Place in the oven for 7 minutes at 165°C (fan).

For The Italian Meringue

Add the sugar and water to a pan and bring to 121°C. Just before reaching this temperature, whisk together the egg whites and lemon juice. Continue to whisk until it forms firm peaks, then pour a steady stream of the syrup into the mix to create a glossy, firm texture. Whisk for 10 minutes. Once cooled, add to a piping bag.

For The Candied Fennel

Bring the water and sugar to the boil. Slice the fennel but keep the root attached, poach in the syrup for 30 minutes until translucent and tender. Allow to cool.

For The Sable Biscuit

Cream the butter and icing sugar, then add the flour, yolks and salt. Roll out and chill for 30 minutes. Cut the pastry into rectangles and bake at 180°C (fan) for 7 minutes.

To Assemble The Dish

Place a biscuit first, then the raspberry parfait on top with the fruits, candied fennel and lemon curd dotted around the plate decoratively. Pipe on the Italian meringue and glaze using a blow torch. Add the yoghurt sorbet and finish with a raspberry tuile.

Chef's Tip

Use fresh produce that's grown and picked on your doorstep; substitute the fruit components of the dish with whatever is ripe and in season.

028
BABUCHO BAR, RESTAURANT & LOUNGE CLUB

26 Side, Lower Dean Street, Newcastle Upon Tyne, NE1 3JD

0191 231 2840
www.babucho.co.uk Twitter: @BabuchoNCL Facebook: Babucho Newcastle Instagram: BabuchoNCL

Following the birth of his first son, founder and managing director Robert Scott opened the vibrant 'Babucho' in 2011. The restaurant name aptly translates as a term for 'Daddy' in Italian, and welcomes fellow Geordies and tourists alike to its opulent candle-lit restaurant booths and cool lounge bar.

A short meander away from the bustling shopping district, take in the breathtaking Newcastle architecture of Grey Street and Dean Street and you will find Babucho nestled in the historic gothic looking gateway to the cosmopolitan quayside area.

Babucho prides itself on its restaurant atmosphere, building a phenomenal reputation for its Italian home style cuisine, delivered with the warmest Geordie welcome. This is fused with the glamour of a cool live DJ set in the sumptuous lounge bar, where guests can sip cocktails until the wee hours.

The key to their success? "Our people", says Robby.

Executive chef Gary Cook has worked globally. His cooking ability is highly skilled and innovative , but it's his ability as a team manager and dedication to motivating, inspiring and training young chefs keen to enter the industry that really sets him apart. Robby, Gary, head chef Chris Cook and general manager Claire Knight have a 12 year working history and share the same goal to propel Babucho forward, with new sites ear marked both locally and abroad.

A New York style Italian brasserie and bar, with a friendly team who remember your name, cocktails just the way you like them, food you go on holiday to find and a soundtrack you will want to buy.

OVEN ROASTED KING PRAWNS WITH GARLIC & CHILLI BUTTER

SERVES 4

🍷 *Gavi di Gavi , La Toledana 2014*
(Italy)

Method

For The King Prawns

Preheat the oven to 200°C (fan).

Peel and de-vein the king prawns. Place the prawns flat on a large oven tray. Drizzle with a good quality olive oil, some rock salt and a touch of lemon juice. Roast for about 5 minutes until the prawns slightly curl and change colour.

For The Sauce

Add the butter, a splash of white wine, garlic, chilli and another squeeze of lemon juice to a saucepan to make a butter *emulsion* sauce - keep moving the pan!

> **Chef's Tip**
>
> To stop your *emulsion* splitting, always put the butter in first before the wine, chilli and garlic. Keep it moving all the time!

For The Garlic Toast

Paint garlic butter on both sides of the bread and grill until the edges become golden brown.

To Serve

Place the warm toast on a plate and top with king prawns in a straight line. Drizzle the sauce over and finish with half a lemon and a sprinkle of chopped parsley.

Ingredients

King Prawns
20 king prawns (size 8/12)
10ml olive oil
rock salt (pinch of)
lemon juice (squeeze of)

Sauce
50g butter
20g chilli (seeds removed, finely sliced)
10g garlic (finely chopped)
30ml white wine (whatever you are drinking)
lemon juice (squeeze of)

Garlic Toast
4 slices bread (ciabatta or similar, lightly toasted)
garlic butter (knob of, melted)

Garnish
2 lemons (halved)
parsley (finely chopped)

CONFIT DUCK WITH VALPOLICELLA & HONEY SAUCE

SERVES 4

 Valpolicella Classico Superiore Ripasso 2012, La Casetta (Italy)

Ingredients

Confit Duck Legs

4 large duck legs
10g Maldon sea salt
10g peppercorns (large pinch of)
5 bay leaves
2 star anise
200g duck fat (or enough to cover)

Valpolicella And Honey Sauce

500ml Valpolicella wine
1 orange (juice of)
100g sugar
2 sticks cinnamon
2 star anise
100ml beef stock
honey (to taste)

To Serve

400g buttery mashed potato

Garnish

8 fresh cherries
4 sprigs thyme

Method

For The Confit Duck Leg (Prepare ahead)

Remove the knuckles from the duck legs.

Place the duck legs, skin-side up, in a single a layer in a deep roasting tray. Sprinkle with salt and rest in the fridge for 24 hours.

Preheat the oven to 150°C (fan).

Remove the legs from the fridge and wash the salt off.

Place the legs in a clean, deep tray with peppercorns, bay leaves and star anise and cover with the duck fat. The legs will need to be completely submerged in the duck fat.

Slowly cook for 3 hours. When the duck is cooked, remove from the fat, allow to cool and store until needed, for up to 4 days.

Chef's Tip

It is important to salt the duck skin for 24 hours.

For The Valpolicella And Honey Sauce

Reduce the wine, orange juice and sugar with the spices until thick. Add the beef stock and remove the spices. Bring back to the boil and add honey to taste.

To Serve

Preheat the oven to 200°C (fan).

Warm the duck legs in the oven for 10 minutes until hot and the skin is crispy.

Spoon a neat *quenelle* of very buttery mashed potato and sit the duck leg to the side. Drizzle the sauce neatly around the plate.

Garnish with 2 cherries and decorate the duck with a small sprig of thyme.

TIRAMISU LICOR 43

SERVES 4

🍷 *Torcolato Beato Bartolomeo, Breganze (Italy)*

Ingredients

Tiramisu

20ml Licor 43 (vanilla liqueur)
5 shots espresso
10ml Marsala
100g chocolate
100ml pasteurised egg yolk
100g caster sugar
200g mascarpone cheese
50ml pasteurised egg white
8 savoiardi biscuits

Garnish

cocoa powder
berries
biscotti

4 glasses

Method

For The Tiramisu (Prepare the day before)

Combine the espresso, Licor 43 and Marsala to make the soaking liquor.

Grate the chocolate and leave it in the fridge.

Whip the sugar and egg yolk to a *sabayon*. It should double in volume, thicken and turn lighter in colour. Add the mascarpone and whip until smooth and thick.

Whip the egg white to a soft peak.

Beat a quarter of the whipped egg white into the mascarpone mixture, then fold in the rest.

Spread a thin layer of the mascarpone mixture over the bottom of a glass.

Quickly drop the savoiardi biscuits into the coffee mix and turn to coat. Place in the glass, sugar side down, and repeat until the bottom of each glass is covered.

Spread on half of the mascarpone, level off, then top with half of the grated chocolate.

Start again with another layer of soaked biscuits. Finally, spread the remaining mascarpone mixture and level off again neatly. Cover and set in the fridge overnight.

To Serve

Top the tiramisu with the remaining grated chocolate and dust with cocoa powder.

> **Chef's Tip**
> Use a good mascarpone cheese and make sure it is at room temperature before adding it to the mixture.

038
THE BAY HORSE
MUSE & CENA

The multi award-winning Bay Horse in Hurworth village near Darlington, serves exceptional fine dining food in a relaxed and friendly setting. It's a firm favourite among locals and visitors alike, with diners travelling from far and wide to enjoy what the restaurant has to offer.

The emphasis is on the finer details of a traditional English pub with hand pulled local ales, cosy corners and a roaring open fire in the colder months.

If you prefer to dine outside there's a beautiful listed walled garden and for special occasions private dining rooms are available. It serves traditional Sunday lunch and has Prix Fixe and French Tuesdays menus.

The head chefs and many of the teams at all three of Marcus and Jonathan's restaurants, worked with Marcus at the Cleveland Tontine. They are advocates for nurturing new talent and have partnered up with the exceptional in subsequent ventures. They brought in the Bay Horse's manager, Adrian Rummel, as a partner at Muse and Peter Huggins later became their partner at Cena.

MUSE CONTINENTAL CAFE

In October 2012, Marcus, Jonathan and Adrian launched Muse, a Continental café situated on the bustling high street in Yarm. Serving breakfast, lunch, afternoon tea and dinner, seven days a week, the menus offer classic, delicious dishes with the emphasis on quality ingredients.

The restaurant also boasts a licensed pavement café, so you can dine al fresco to enjoy a real Parisian café experience while you watch the world go by.

If you love a great Sunday lunch, you definitely need to try Muse's between 12 and 4pm. The restaurant also has an early bird and 'Prix Fixe' menu and, with its fantastic open plan layout, Muse is ideal for large parties of eight or more, corporate dining and families.

Only a year after opening, Muse became the first restaurant on Yarm High Street to feature in the Michelin Guide. It's also featured in the Top 50 'Fit for Foodies' restaurants in the UK.

CENA TRATTORIA

Cena is Marcus and Jonathan's latest business venture, also on the high street in Yarm. They opened it in June 2014, in partnership with Peter Huggins, who previously managed Muse.

If you're a fan of authentic, Italian cuisine you need look no further than this fabulous, characterful eatery. The chefs cook pizzas in a traditional, wood stone oven and make pasta by hand, fresh every day. The ingredients are imported direct from Italy with dishes made to old fashioned Italian recipes with a twist. All the wines are carefully selected from Latin countries.

The decor makes you feel as if you're in Italy with hard wood floors, reclaimed wooden tables, brightly coloured chairs, white washed beams and a panelled dining room upstairs. Fresh herbs and lavender adorn the restaurant throughout. The bar area features Italian mosaic tiles, antique mirrored glass and a shabby chic, red leather sofa.

Cena is available for private parties on Sundays and, if you're a spur of the moment person, you don't always need to book at Cena so tables are available for walk-in diners.

Marcus took over The Bay Horse at Hurworth, near Darlington, in late 2008 with his old friend and business partner, Jonathan Hall. The pair have since jointly opened two more restaurants - Muse, a continental café, and then Cena, an Italian trattoria, both in Yarm.

Cena Trattoria

HAM HOCK CROQUETTES, ENGLISH MUSTARD CREAM, BROWN SAUCE

Muse Continental Café

104b High Street, Yarm, TS15 9AU

01642 788 558 www.museyarm.com Twitter: @museyarm Facebook: museyarm

SERVES 4

 *Unwooded Chardonnay 2013 Groote Post,
Darling Hills (South Africa)*

Ingredients

Ham Hock
1 raw ham hock
1 onion (peeled), 1 head garlic
2 carrots, 2 sticks celery
1 sprig thyme, 1 bay leaf
5 litres water

Ham Hock Croquettes
1 onion (finely diced)
100g mashed potatoes
500g ham hock (chopped)
1 handful parsley (chopped)
salt and pepper
breadcrumbs (to coat)

Brown Sauce (Makes 750ml)
285ml water, 285ml red wine vinegar
142ml tomato juice, 250ml maple syrup
60ml orange juice, 100g dates
70ml cider vinegar, 3 tbsp treacle
3 tbsp tamarind pulp, 45ml apple juice
½ tsp onion powder, ½ tsp whole cloves
½ cardamom pod, ½ tsp black pepper
½ tsp powdered garlic, ½ tsp mustard seeds
1 tsp sea salt, 1½cm cinnamon stick

English Mustard Cream
175ml double cream
3 tsp English mustard
2 tsp shallot (diced), 1 tsp caster sugar
2 tsp white wine vinegar
salt (pinch of)

To Serve
25ml oil, 4 eggs
butter (knob of), salt and pepper
oyster mushrooms (sautéed), chervil
caperberries

Method

For The Ham Hock

Chop all the vegetables roughly and place in a pan with the ham hock. Pour over the water, bring to the boil and simmer for 4 hours, topping up the water to cover if needed. Remove the ham hock and pull the meat off the bone. Strain the vegetables from the stock and discard them.

> **Chef's Tip**
>
> Pick the meat from the ham hock while it's still warm as it will fall straight off the bone.

For The Ham Hock Croquettes

Fry the onions until soft, then mix with the mashed potato, ham and parsley. Season to taste. Form into 4 croquettes and roll in breadcrumbs.

For The Brown Sauce

Place all of the ingredients in a pan and simmer for 1 hour, leave to rest. Purée and pass through a sieve.

For The English Mustard Cream

Whip the cream to thicken it slightly. Mix all the rest of the ingredients together and fold into the cream.

To Serve

Preheat the oven to 180°C (fan).

Deep fry (160°C) the croquettes for 5 minutes until golden, then place into the oven for 5 minutes.

Heat the oil in a frying pan for 2 minutes. Crack in 1 egg at a time, spoon the oil over the eggs, add the butter and spoon over. Season with a pinch of salt and a pinch of black pepper. Remove from the pan and place on a chopping board. Cut away the excess egg white. Place the ham croquette on a plate and top with the fried egg. Place a *quenelle* of mustard cream to the side and decorate with a few dots of homemade brown sauce. Scatter with a few caperberries and sautéed oyster mushrooms and top with chervil.

GROUSE, GROUSE HASH CAKE, BREAD SAUCE, REDCURRANT JELLY, CELERIAC PUREE

The Bay Horse
45 The Green, Hurworth, Darlington, Durham, DL2 2AA
01325 720 663 www.thebayhorsehurworth.com

SERVES 4

 Château Beaumont 2010 Haut Medoc (France)

Ingredients

Grouse
4 grouse (legs removed and reserved)
butter (knob of, softened), salt and pepper

Redcurrant Jelly
200g fresh redcurrants (well washed)
water (to cover), sugar (115g per 190ml liquid)
agar agar (1g per 100ml liquid)

Grouse Hash Cake
8 grouse legs (rubbed with oil, sprinkled with salt)
300g sausagemeat
1 onion, 1 carrot, 1 clove garlic (peeled, finely diced)
butter (knob of), 1 tbsp seed mustard
1 tsp redcurrant jelly, 25g parsley (chopped)
flour, beaten egg, breadcrumbs (to *pane*)

Bread Sauce
450ml milk, 75g butter, 2 cloves
1 bay leaf (crumbled)
1 sprig thyme, salt (good pinch of)
1 small onion (finely chopped), 3 tbsp double cream
110g fresh white breadcrumbs, pepper

Port And Cranberry Sauce
2 tbsp cranberry jelly
½ large orange, ½ small lemon (zest and juice of)
1 tsp root ginger (grated), 1 tsp English mustard
3 tbsp port, 568ml reduced chicken stock

Celeriac Purée
1 medium celeriac (peeled), 100ml full-fat milk
100ml double cream, 1g caster sugar, 1g salt

Game Crumbs
75g butter, 75g fresh white breadcrumbs
55ml medium dry sherry, salt and pepper

To Serve
1 small celeriac (diced, tossed in oil, salted)
spinach (wilted with butter, salt and pepper)

Method

For The Grouse
Preheat the oven to 200°C (fan).
Rub the grouse with butter and season. Brown all over, then oven cook for 8 minutes. Rest upside down for 10 minutes.

For The Redcurrant Jelly (Prepare the day before)
Boil the redcurrants in water until tender. Suspend a jelly bag or several layers of muslin in a sieve over a bowl. Pour a little boiling water through and discard. Pour in the contents of the saucepan. Leave to drip overnight.
Simmer the juice with sugar for 10 minutes. Leave to cool.
Add the agar agar and bring to the boil. Set in a lined container. Cut into dice.

For The Grouse Hash Cake
Preheat the oven to 170°C (fan).
Roast the legs and sausagemeat for 30 minutes. Pick the leg meat, mix with the sausagemeat and chop finely. Sweat the vegetables and garlic in a little butter until soft. Combine all the ingredients, roll into 25g cakes and *pane*. Deep fry at 160°C for 2 minutes.

For The Bread Sauce
Heat the milk, butter, cloves, herbs, salt and onion to just below boiling point. Simmer extremely gently for 10 minutes. Remove from the heat, cover and leave to infuse. Strain the milk into a clean pan. Reheat gently with the cream and whisk in the breadcrumbs. Allow to thicken. Season.

For The Port And Cranberry Sauce
Simmer all the ingredients for 10 minutes. Infuse for 1 hour. Bring back to the boil, simmer for 2 minutes. Pass through a fine sieve.

For The Celeriac Purée
Dice the celeriac into 1cm pieces. Simmer the ingredients for 30 minutes until soft and the milk almost evaporated. Blend, then pass through a fine sieve.

For The Game Crumbs
Colour the butter in a large pan. When nut brown, add the crumbs, stirring until golden. Add the sherry and stir until evaporated, breaking up the crumb. Season.

To Serve
Bake the celeriac dice for 7 minutes. Carve the breasts off the grouse, remove the skin and place on top of the spinach. Pour any resting juices into the sauce and drizzle over the breasts. Add all the other elements as pictured.

BANANA SUNDAE

Cena Trattoria

85 High Street, Yarm, Stockton-on-Tees, TS15 9AH
01642 780 088 www.cenayarm.com Twitter: @cenayarm Facebook: Cena - Yarm

SERVES 4

Moscato d'Asti, Bera, Piemonte
(Italy)

Ingredients

Banana Parfait

8 egg yolks, 150ml cold water
450g caster sugar, 4 egg whites
salt (small pinch of), 300ml double cream
3 very ripe bananas (mashed)
2 tbsp Crème de Banane (or white rum)

Chocolate Brownie Base

2 medium eggs, 175g caster sugar
340g bitter chocolate (chopped)
150g butter (melted)
1 vanilla pod (seeds of)
60g plain flour (sieved), 20g cocoa powder
½ tsp baking powder, 100g hazelnuts

Malt Chocolate Ice Cream

500ml full-fat milk
40g cocoa powder (sieved)
135g caster sugar
1½ tsp vanilla essence
340ml whipping cream
115g Horlicks

Fudge Sauce

50ml golden syrup, 40g caster sugar
50ml water, 25g cocoa powder
120g plain chocolate (melted)

Vanilla Cream

500ml cream, 50g caster sugar
1 vanilla pod (seeds of)

Caramelised Bananas

1 banana, sugar (to coat)

To Serve

4 tbsp Baileys, 1 banana (chopped)
almond flakes (chopped, toasted)

terrine mould (lined with cling film)
12cm x 36cm baking tray (lined)
4 sundae dishes

Method

For The Banana Parfait (Prepare ahead)

Make a *pâte á bombe* by mixing the yolks, water and 200g of sugar in a stainless steel bowl. Sit over a pan of simmering water and cook, stirring frequently until thick enough to support the spoon upright in the centre. It may take up to 1 hour. Remove from the heat, allow to cool slightly then push through a fine sieve into a clean bowl and beat until cool, light and fluffy. Whisk the egg whites with the remaining 250g of caster sugar and salt in a mixer until it resembles shaving foam. Whisk into the *pâte á bombe* in 2 stages.

Whip the cream to the same consistency as the meringue and pâte mix, then combine. Finally, whisk in the mashed banana and liqueur, pour into the terrine mould and freeze.

For The Chocolate Brownie Base

Preheat the oven to 180°C (fan).

Whisk the eggs and sugar until pale. Melt 240g of the chocolate, then stir in the butter and vanilla seeds. Fold in the egg mix followed by the flour, cocoa and baking powder. Stir in the nuts and pour into the lined baking tray. Bake for 25 minutes.

For The Malt Chocolate Ice Cream

Bring the milk, cocoa and sugar to the boil, mix well. Simmer gently for 5 minutes. Chill in the fridge. When cool, blend in a food processor with the vanilla essence, cream and Horlicks. Strain, then churn in an ice cream machine.

For The Fudge Sauce

Place the golden syrup, sugar, water and cocoa powder in a pan and boil for 2 minutes. Finally, add the melted chocolate.

For The Vanilla Cream

Place a bowl in the freezer for 10 minutes. Pour all the ingredients into the chilled bowl and whisk to soft peaks.

For The Caramelised Bananas

Trim the bananas into squares. Dip into sugar and caramelise with a blow torch.

> **Chef's Tip**
> Never pick the caramelised bananas up straight after caramelising.

To Serve

Place some chopped up brownie in the bottom of a sundae dish and sprinkle with Baileys. Top with some squares of banana parfait and chopped banana. Pour in 2 tablespoons of fudge sauce, then 2 scoops of malt chocolate ice cream. Top with vanilla cream and almond flakes. Garnish with caramelised bananas.

BISTRO ROMANO

63 Front Street, Cleadon Village, Sunderland, Tyne & Wear, SR6 7PG

0191 519 1747
www.bistroromano.co.uk

Bistro Romano lies in the heart of Cleadon Village and is owned by brothers Romano and Paolo Minchella who have been in the restaurant trade for over 30 years. Growing up within an Italian background, Romano and Paolo started their journey working within the family award-winning ice cream business. In 1971 Romano won the International Ice Cream Competition in Paris and a decade later the brothers decided to open their first restaurant 'Romanos' in Seaburn. After 20 years of operating successful restaurants in the local area, the brothers opened the elegant Bistro in 1999.

Bistro Romano has long been considered a destination restaurant and is much loved by the local community. The menu offers good honest cuisine with a strong Italian influence. The restaurant has built a reputation for providing the best quality seasonal produce, good service and delicious food in a relaxed and friendly atmosphere.

The kitchen is headed by Lee Jackson and his dedicated team who are passionate about sourcing local and sustainable produce and using the finest ingredients in each dish.

They also stock an extensive range of wines from the around the world and a fantastic range of specialised spirits, cognacs and grappe. Open seven days a week for lunch and dinner. Traditional lunch on Sundays.

Bistro Romano has built its reputation on providing real, honest, flavoursome food. Cooking techniques used have been passed down through family traditions and provide the basis on which every dish is prepared.

LINGUINE ALLE VONGOLE

SERVES 4

 Gavi di Gavi, Marchesi di Barolo, 2014
(Italy)

Ingredients

500g small, fresh palourde clams
120g linguine

Sauce

50ml olive oil
2-3 cloves garlic (chopped)
1 fresh chilli (finely chopped)
4 anchovy fillets (finely chopped)
50ml white wine
parsley (handful of, chopped)

To Serve

extra virgin olive oil (drizzle of)

Method

To Prepare The Clams

Soak the clams in cold water for 15-20 minutes to remove any residue sand. Lift out, place in a sieve and shake under cold running water. Leave to dry.

For The Linguine

Cook the linguine in salted, boiling water for 10-12 minutes until 'al dente'. Drain when ready.

For The Sauce

Heat the olive oil in a pan. Gently fry the garlic, chilli and anchovies until the anchovies melt into the oil. Add the clams and white wine. Cover and cook until clams start to open. Discard any unopened clams. Turn up the heat, reduce any excess liquid, then add the pasta and chopped parsley. Toss and serve with a drizzle of extra virgin olive oil.

To Serve

Serve as pictured.

> #### Chef's Tip
>
> For a richer sauce, add a generous knob of butter while tossing the pasta towards the end.

PAN FRIED HALIBUT, ROAST MEDITERRANEAN VEGETABLES, SHALLOT & TOMATO DRESSING

SERVES 4

 *I Frati Lugana Cà dei Frati 2014
(Italy)*

Ingredients

Halibut

4 x 200g halibut portions (skinless)
25g butter
20ml olive oil
sea salt (pinch of)

Mediterranean Vegetables

1 red pepper
1 green pepper
1 yellow pepper
1 red onion
1 courgette
1 small aubergine
4-5 cloves garlic
80ml olive oil
sea salt (large sprinkling of)

Shallot And Tomato Dressing

3 tomatoes
2 banana shallots (peeled)
40ml olive oil
20ml white wine
sea salt (pinch of)

Method

For Mediterranean Vegetables

Preheat the oven to 200°C.

Roughly dice all the vegetables to the same size. Peel the garlic and cut the cloves in half. Spread all the vegetables evenly on a baking tray and generously season with sea salt and olive oil. Toss the vegetables to ensure they are well coated. Bake for 8-10 minutes until soft, shaking the tray regularly.

> **Chef's Tip**
>
> Before preparation, make sure all the vegetables have been thoroughly washed and dried to avoid excess moisture.

For The Shallot And Tomato Dressing

Blanch the tomatoes for 10 seconds in salted, boiling water. Refresh in cold water. Skin the tomatoes, then cut them in half and deseed. Finely dice the tomatoes and shallots.

Heat the olive oil in a frying pan and sauté the shallots until lightly brown. Add the tomatoes and white wine and cook until reduced. Season to taste.

For The Halibut

Heat the olive oil in a non-stick frying pan. Place the fish in the pan and lightly season with sea salt. Leave until lightly browned. Flip the halibut, add a little sea salt to the other side and a small knob of butter. Place the pan under a hot grill for 3-4 minutes until cooked.

To Serve

Serve as pictured.

LIME & GINGER CHEESECAKE

SERVES 8

 Passito di Noto, Planeta
(Italy)

Ingredients

Cheesecake Base
1 packet ginger biscuits
50g butter (melted)

Cheesecake Filling
175g mascarpone
75g cream cheese
300ml whipping cream
100g caster sugar
2-3 limes (juice and zest of)

Ginger Sauce
30g root ginger (peeled)
100ml water
50g caster sugar

20cm cheesecake ring

Method

For The Cheesecake Base

Crush the ginger biscuits, making sure you don't crush them too fine. Stir in the melted butter and mix until all the crumbs are coated. Place a cheesecake ring on greaseproof paper. Press the crumbs into the ring and smooth out with a spoon. Place in the fridge until cold.

For The Filling

Place the mascarpone, cream cheese, whipping cream and sugar in a large bowl. Mix until well combined and smooth in texture. Add the lime juice and zest and whisk thoroughly. Place the mix into the ring and smooth out. Return to the fridge.

Chef's Tip

If you would like more zing, add the juice of half a lemon to the cheesecake mix.

For The Ginger Sauce

Finely dice the ginger and place in a pan with the water and sugar. Simmer until the sauce thickens. Remove from the heat and cool.

To Serve

Serve as pictured.

058
THE BLACK BULL INN

Moulton, Richmond, North Yorkshire, DL10 6QJ

01325 377 556
www.theblackbullmoulton.com Twitter: @Black_bull_2013

This iconic pub has been synonymous with good food and wine for many years. Following a period of neglect, Provenance Inns & Hotels rescued this historic dining pub and undertook an extensive refurbishment and modernisation. Now re-established to its former glory, The Black Bull re-opened to critical acclaim in April 2014. The inn retains the classic bar and tap room, and now has a 120 cover restaurant. There are three exclusive private dining areas, including the fantastic James Herriot Suite - a large, sophisticated, light and airy private dining room, with log fire, Champagne bar and terrace.

The Provenance Inns' team provides an exceptionally friendly welcome and celebrate the very best in Yorkshire's local produce from both land and sea. The county's farmers and producers are championed in every aspect of the Black Bull's award-winning food; from delicious fish and chips with a pint in the cosy traditional bar, to a gourmet dining experience or a family Sunday lunch in the restaurant.

Pride in Provenance... from field to fork the provenance of our food and drink is at the heart of all we do at the award-winning Black Bull Inn, Moulton.

CRISPY APPLE & CHORIZO BLACK PUDDING, TARRAGON HOLLANDAISE & HERITAGE TOMATO

SERVES 4

 Gewurztraminer 'Beblenheim' 2013, Domaine Trapet (Alsace, France)

Ingredients

Apple And Chorizo Black Pudding

125ml white wine vinegar
1 sprig thyme
125g caster sugar
2 shallots (finely diced)
1 clove garlic (minced)
5 rashers streaky bacon (roughly chopped)
1 cooking apple (grated)
250g blood mix (blood, barley and oatmeal - available from local butchers)
180g pork back fat (finely diced)
80g Three Little Pigs Rare Breed Yorkshire chorizo
140ml warm water

Heritage Tomato Chutney

125g red onions (finely sliced)
1 red chilli (deseeded, sliced)
2 cloves garlic (finely minced)
500g heritage tomatoes (roughly chopped)
1 sprig thyme
70g Demerara sugar
40ml red wine vinegar

Tarragon Hollandaise

200ml white wine vinegar
1 shallot (minced)
6 black peppercorns
1 bay leaf
25g fresh tarragon (plus 1 sprig)
2 free range egg yolks
125g *clarified* unsalted butter
½ lemon (juice of), salt and pepper

Pane Mix

100g fine breadcrumbs, 50g plain flour (seasoned)
1 large free range egg (beaten)

flan dish (lined with cling film)

Method

For The Apple And Chorizo Black Pudding (Prepare the day before)

Simmer the vinegar with the thyme and sugar until reduced by half, pass through a sieve.

Slowly cook the shallots, garlic, bacon and apple in a pan until soft, but not coloured. Place the blood mix, fat, chorizo and bacon mix into a large bowl, add the vinegar reduction and warm water and mix thoroughly.

Preheat the oven to 160°C.

Place the mix into the flan dish and completely wrap tightly with cling film ensuring it is sealed. Place in a tray of warm water and bake for 45 minutes. Once cooked, remove from the water bath and allow to cool. Refrigerate overnight.

> **Chef's Tip**
>
> Making your own black pudding is to go the extra mile however the flavours will certainly impress! The apple can be substituted for apricot if you prefer.

For The Heritage Tomato Chutney

Slowly cook the onions, chilli and garlic in a pan until soft. Add the chopped tomatoes and thyme, simmer for 10 minutes. Stir in the sugar and vinegar, cook to a thick sauce consistency.

For The Tarragon Hollandaise

Reduce the vinegar with the shallot, peppercorns, bay leaf and sprig of tarragon to 90ml.

Place the vinegar reduction and egg yolks into a metal bowl over a pan of simmering water, whisk until the mixture starts to thicken. Remove from the heat and whisk in the *clarified butter* until the mixture *emulsifies*. Add the remaining tarragon, season with the lemon juice, adding salt and pepper to taste.

To Serve

Cut the black pudding into 1cm x 4cm lengths, *pane*, then deep fry. Serve immediately, assembling as pictured.

HOT HOME SMOKED SALMON, CHARRED AUBERGINE & LEEKS, CARAMELISED SHALLOT POTATO & RED WINE JUS

SERVES 4

 Guardiola Bianco 2013, Tenuta di Passopisciaro, Sicily (Italy)

Ingredients

Smoked Salmon

4 x 150g fresh salmon fillets
rock salt
50g oak wood chippings
25g muscovado sugar

Caramelised Shallot Potato

30ml vegetable oil
20g unsalted butter
2 banana shallots (finely sliced)
1 clove garlic (minced)
2 sprigs fresh thyme (picked)
325g Maris Piper potatoes (peeled)
salt and cracked black pepper

Aubergine Purée

1 medium aubergine
1 clove garlic (chopped)
20ml olive oil
20g ground cumin
1 sprig thyme
1 sprig rosemary
25g unsalted butter
salt and pepper

Red Wine Jus

2 tbsp olive oil
2 medium shallots (peeled, finely sliced)
2 sprigs thyme1 bay leaf
3-4 white and black peppercorns (crushed)
1 bottle red wine
2½ litres good quality veal stock

Garnish

4 heads pak choi (outer leaves wilted)
8 baby leeks (chargrilled)

6cm pastry ring

Method

For The Smoked Salmon

Place the salmon portions on a tray and completely cover in rock salt. Leave for 30 minutes, wash the salt off and dry the salmon. Preheat the oven to 180°C.

Line a deep, metal tray with tin foil. Add the wood chippings mixed with the sugar. Heat on the stove until the wood starts to smoke. Place the salmon, flesh side down, onto a cooling rack and then transfer into the tray, ensuring the fish does not touch the wood chippings. Tightly cover with tin foil, lower the heat and smoke for 7 minutes. Remove the salmon, place on a tray and bake for 8-10 minutes.

> **Chef's Tip**
> Any type of wood chips can be used for home smoking - try maple, hickory or applewood.

For The Caramelised Shallot Potato

Heat a tablespoon of vegetable oil with the butter in a heavy bottomed saucepan until it foams. Add the shallots, garlic and thyme, cook over a low to medium heat until deeply golden in colour. Remove from the heat and allow to cool. Preheat the oven to 180°C.

Coarsely grate the potatoes into a bowl and squeeze out any excess water with a clean cloth. Add the shallot mixture to the grated potato, mix and season with salt and pepper. Divide the potato into 4 and shape using the pastry ring. Seal in a hot pan with the remaining oil. Bake for 12 minutes.

For The Aubergine Purée

Preheat the oven to 180°C.

Halve the aubergine lengthways, score the flesh and place onto a very hot griddle pan until chargrilled. Place on a tray, skin-side down, sprinkle over the chopped garlic, olive oil, ground cumin, thyme and rosemary. Seal the tray with tin foil and bake for 45 minutes until soft. Remove the herb sprigs and scoop out the centre of the aubergine. Blitz to a smooth purée with the butter. Season to taste.

For The Red Wine Jus

Heat the oil in a pan. When hot, fry the shallots until lightly browned. Add the herbs and black pepper, stir frequently for 3 minutes. Pour in the wine and reduce by two thirds, add the stock and again reduce by two thirds. Strain the jus and keep warm.

To Serve

Assemble as pictured.

CHOCOLATE & PEANUT INDULGENCE

SERVES 4

🍷 *San Emilio Pedro Ximénez NV, Solera Reserva, Emilio Lustau, Jerez, (Spain)*

Ingredients

Baileys 'Magnum'

3 medium, free range eggs
1 free range egg yolk
80g caster sugar
25ml Baileys
280ml double cream (whipped to soft peaks)
50g 53.5% dark chocolate (melted)

Chocolate Crunch

70g 53.5% dark chocolate
40g unsalted butter
30ml golden syrup
50g Rice Krispies
50g white chocolate

Chocolate Mousse

75g 53.5% dark chocolate
15ml full-fat milk
2 free range egg yolks
25g caster sugar
1 tbsp praline paste
125ml double cream (whipped to soft peaks)

Hot Chocolate Fondant

100g unsalted butter
4 tsp cocoa powder
100g 53.5% dark chocolate
2 medium, free range eggs
2 free range egg yolks
120g caster sugar
100g plain flour

Garnish

peanut brittle
peanut ice cream

4 lolly moulds
4 x 5cm ramekins

Method

For The Baileys 'Magnum'

Place the eggs, yolk and sugar in a bowl and whisk to stiff peaks to a *sabayon*. Fold in the Baileys, then the whipped cream. Pour into ice lolly moulds with popsicle sticks and freeze. Once frozen, remove from the mould, dip in 'just melted' dark chocolate and freeze once more.

For The Chocolate Crunch

Melt 50g of dark chocolate over a pan of simmering water. Remove from the heat, then add the butter and golden syrup, mix well. Add the Rice Krispies to the chocolate mix, roll into small balls and leave to set on a tray in the fridge. Once set, dip the balls into the white chocolate (melted) and return to the refrigerator to set. Melt the remaining dark chocolate and drizzle over the top.

For The Chocolate Mousse

Melt the dark chocolate in the milk over a pan of simmering water. Whisk the egg yolks and caster sugar to stiff peaks in a separate bowl, then whisk in the praline paste. Fold the melted chocolate mixture into the *sabayon*, add the whipped cream and mix well. Place in the refrigerator for 2-3 hours until set.

For The Hot Chocolate Fondant

Preheat the oven to 180°C.

Butter the ramekins and dust liberally with the cocoa powder, shake out the excess. Melt the dark chocolate and butter in a bowl over a pan of hot water. Take off the heat and stir until smooth. Leave to cool for 10 minutes. Using an electric whisk, beat the eggs, yolks and sugar until pale and thick, incorporate the chocolate mixture. Sift the flour and gently fold in. Divide between the ramekins and bake for 8 minutes.

> **Chef's Tip**
> Be careful to time the cooking of the chocolate fondants exactly; this may vary slightly dependent on your oven. Remove when the tops are just set.

To Plate

Assemble as pictured.

068
THE BRUCE ARMS

Main Street, West Tanfield, Ripon North Yorkshire, HG4 5JJ

01677 470 325
www.thebrucearms.com

The Bruce Arms in the centre of the historic village of West Tanfield, is an 18th Century coaching inn which serviced the route through Wensleydale, 'over the top' to Kendal in the Lake District.

The horse drawn coaches may be long gone but the stable yard and the walls of the old inn, sketched by JMW Turner in 1816, are steeped in the character of that bygone era. However, having been recently refurbished, the style of the interior - which includes three guest bedrooms, a characterful bar and dining area with log burning stove and a private dining room for 30 diners - fits very well into the 21st Century.

Chefs Dave Mathews and Lee Costello take real pride in producing dishes which also reflect their Yorkshire heritage as well as being very contemporary. Both have worked and trained in some of the best restaurants in the north of England.

Their frequently changing menu is designed for classic three or four course meals but it also includes sharing platters for informal dining, as well as sandwiches and salads for lighter lunches. There's always plenty of local game, North Sea fish and locally reared meat to choose from.

The Bruce is very much a family affair since the chefs' wives, Maggie and Crystal, run the front of house and owner Gil Richardson is Maggie's aunt. Various other family members help out regularly.

Dave has worked with Gil for many years and is involved in the kitchen at the sister establishment, The Bull Inn, which is on the banks of the River Ure, also in West Tanfield. Dave and the chef at The Bull, Graham Camsey, have produced a traditional pub menu for this busy local which has the same hallmarks of quality that have been established at The Bruce Arms.

Warning!

KAMIKAZE PEARS
OVERHEAD

IF YOU SIT ON THE
TERRACE, WE CANNOT
BE RESPONSIBLE FOR
RUINED HAIRDOS, BRUISES
OR A KINKY FLAVOUR
SQUASHED PEAR IN
OF YOUR DRINKS
....

(But, there a
nice, so it might be worth
rich!)

THE BRUCE ARMS
RESTAURANT PUB ROOMS

Visit our website
for upcoming events &
special offers

www.thebrucearm...

Here in West Tanfield, you can enjoy
Yorkshire hospitality at its very best; in
the atmosphere of a traditional local at
The Bull Inn or with informal, quality
dining at 'The Bruce'.

"Keeping One's
Guests Supplied
With. Liquor Is
The First Law Of
Hospitality"

CHEF SHOT RABBIT TERRINE

SERVES 4

 Grüner Veltliner, Gobelsburger, Schloss Gobelsburg (Austria)
Forget the old 'anti-freeze scandal' of the eighties, this elegant and aromatic white with spice and pepper notes, matches wonderfully and shows how magical Austrian wines are.

Ingredients

Confit Rabbit

4 rabbits (dressed)
duck fat (enough to cover)
5 cloves garlic
3 bay leaves
3 sprigs rosemary
3 sprigs thyme

Terrine

15ml sherry vinegar
10 sprigs parsley (finely chopped)
salt and pepper (to season)
750g butter
3 shallots (diced)
2 cloves garlic (crushed, finely chopped)
2 purple heritage carrots
2 yellow heritage carrots

Boozy Prunes

125g pitted prunes
2 star anise
100ml Madeira
100ml port

Pickled Walnuts

125g walnuts
2 star anise
2 bay leaves
200ml white wine vinegar
200g caster sugar

Garnish

1 leek (finely sliced into strips)
endive

terrine mould

Method

For The Confit Rabbit

Preheat the oven to 120ºC.

Place the rabbit into a deep casserole pot and add the *confit* ingredients. Cook for 3½ hours. Allow to cool slightly, lift out and drain.

For The Terrine

Remove the *confit* rabbit meat from the bone and place into a large mixing bowl. Add the vinegar and chopped parsley and season. Sweat the shallots and garlic in a little butter, then add to the *confit* rabbit. *Blanch* the carrots separately in salted, boiling water for 5-7 minutes until tender. Remove and cool in iced water. Quarter lengthways.

To Make The Terrine (Prepare the day before)

Grease the terrine mould with olive oil and line with 3 layers of cling film, leaving enough overhang to wrap the terrine. Place the first even layer of rabbit mix into the mould. Alternate with coloured carrots on the next level and continue layering until full. Ensure the top layer is rabbit. Tightly pull across the overhanging cling film, wrap and make sure there are no leaks. Weigh it down, press and chill in the fridge overnight.

For The Boozy Prunes

Place the ingredients in a pan, bring to the boil and simmer until the prunes are plump. Cool and refrigerate.

For The Pickled Walnuts

Place all the ingredients in a pan and reduce to a syrup. Cool.

For The Garnish

Blanch the leeks in boiling, salted water for 20 seconds, then plunge into iced water and drain. Deep fry the leeks, stirring constantly, ensuring they are evenly coloured. Remove and drain well.

To Serve

Portion the terrine by slicing across. Place in the centre of the plate. Alternate the boozy prunes and pickled walnuts around the terrine, placing the crispy leeks and endive in the gaps between.

Chef's Tip

Bearing in mind this is a cold starter, it may be necessary to slightly over season since the chill can dull down the effect of the seasoning.

PAN ROASTED NIDDERDALE PARTRIDGE, BOULANGERE POTATO, POACHED WILLIAMS PEAR

SERVES 4

🍷 *Château Vieux Peyrouquet, Saint-Emilion,*
Bordeaux (France)
This dish cries out for something traditional but not
too heavy. Partridge, being lighter than pheasant,
can often be overpowered.

Ingredients

Partridge

2 whole dressed partridge
100ml chicken stock

Boulangère Potato

6 large, red skin potatoes (finely sliced)
1 large white onion (finely sliced)
300ml reduced chicken stock
250g butter
2 cloves
2 sprigs fresh thyme
salt and white pepper (to taste)

Poached Pear

2 Williams pears (peeled, cored)
red wine (enough to cover)
1 bay leaf
3 juniper berries
½ stick cinnamon
1 orange (zest and juice of)
1 star anise
30ml honey

Lardons, Sprouts And Panko Breadcrumb

100g bacon (about 6 rashers, cut into lardons)
16 Brussel sprouts (outer leaves removed)
150g panko breadcrumbs
2 sprigs parsley (chopped)
100ml veal jus (reduced veal stock)
100g prepared, cooked chestnuts
salt and pepper (to taste)
butter and oil (to fry)

Method

For The Partridge

Remove the legs from the birds and set aside.

For The Partridge Leg Lollipops

Cut the legs in half between the drumstick and thigh. Retaining the drumstick, *French trim*, roll and wrap in cling film. Cook in chicken stock for about 8 minutes. Set aside to cool.

For The Boulangère Potatoes (Prepare 1 day in advance)

Preheat the oven to 160°C.

Sweat the onion, garlic and thyme in a little butter. Add the stock and reduce until viscous. Gently melt the butter and pour over the potatoes. Layer the potatoes in an ovenproof dish, alternating with the onion and stock mix. Bake for 1½ hours until tender. Press with a weight using a tray that fits inside the dish. Leave to cool, then portion into rectangles, approximately 3cm x 10cm.

For The Poached Pear

Place all the ingredients in a pan and simmer until the pears are tender. Cool and place to one side.

For The Bacon Lardons

Sauté in butter until lightly coloured.

For The Brussel Sprouts

Cook in boiling, salted water until tender. Cool in iced water.

For The Panko Breadcrumb

Fry the breadcrumbs in butter until crispy and golden. Season to taste, then stir in the parsley and set aside.

To Serve

Preheat the oven to 220°C.

Heat an ovenproof pan, add a little oil and butter and sear the partridge crown until lightly coloured. Place in the oven for 7-10 minutes. Rest for 2-3 minutes, then remove the breasts. Reheat the boulangère potato by sautéing in butter. Reheat the legs in the veal jus, then dip into the panko breadcrumb mix, cleaning any residue from the bone. Reheat the bacon, chestnuts, sprouts and pear in a little butter. Assemble as pictured.

> **Chef's Tip**
>
> Because of the number of components in this dish, good organisation is key to success. Do not overcook the crown as partridge has a tendency to become quite tough. The resting of the breasts is crucial.

MULLED PEAR TART TATIN WITH MAPLE & WALNUT ICE CREAM

SERVES 4

Red Muscadel, Nuy Winery (South Africa)
With quite a bit going on in this dish, a wine with
structure is required, so our choice would be this
inspiring Red Muscadel.

Ingredients

Mulled Pears

8 Williams pears (peeled, cored)
1 bottle red wine
2 star anise
1 stick cinnamon
6 juniper berries
2 oranges (zest and juice of)
250g caster sugar
200ml honey

Tart Tatin

350g caster sugar
2 tbsp cold water
1 sheet ready rolled puff pastry (cut into a disc
1cm larger than the tart tatin pan)

Maple And Walnut Ice Cream

500ml of semi-skimmed milk
130g caster sugar
20ml vanilla extract
8 medium eggs
100g walnuts (crushed)
200ml maple syrup

Garnish

spun sugar
soft fruits
biscuit crumb

23cm wide, heavy bottomed, ovenproof frying pan

Method

For The Mulled Pears

Place all the ingredients in a pan, bring to the boil and simmer for 20 minutes. Cover with a *cartouche* and leave to cool in the liquor. Drain and dry the pears, then slice.

For The Tart Tatin

Place the sugar and water into a heavy bottomed pan and heat gently until caramelised, then pour into the wide, oven proof frying pan to cool. Arrange the sliced pears in and around the caramel in the pan, then place the pastry over the top. Crimp the edges of the pastry.

Preheat the oven to 220°C.

Bake in the oven for 20-25 minutes until crisp and golden. When cooked, allow to cool for 2-3 minutes before turning out.

To turn out, cover the pan with a larger plate and carefully flip over. Allow a few moments for the tart tatin to release and lift away from the pan.

For The Maple And Walnut Ice Cream

Heat the milk, vanilla extract and sugar in a pan, bring to the boil and simmer. Whisk the eggs in a bowl and pour one third of the milk mix into the eggs, whisking continuously. Pour the egg mix back into the pan, stirring continuously until the mixture lightly coats the back of the spoon. Allow to cool. Pour the crème Anglaise, walnuts and maple syrup into an ice cream machine and churn.

Chef's Tip

If you do not have an ice cream maker, place your mixture into the freezer in a container and stir every 20 minutes until lightly frozen. Freeze as normal.

To Serve

Quarter the tart tatin and serve with a *quenelle* of ice cream. Garnish with fruit and spun sugar. If necessary, to stop the ice cream sliding around the plate, set the *quenelle* on a base of a few sweet biscuit crumbs.

078
CAFE LILLI

83 High Street, Norton, Stockton on Tees, TS20 1AE

01642 554 422
www.lillicafe.co.uk Twitter: @cafelilli Facebook: Café Lilli Instagram: cafelilli10

Owner Roberto Pittalis was born on the beautiful Island of Sardinia, in the city of Sassari, where his love of good food and fine wine started at a very early age. He used to help his grandparents on their farm picking the fresh produce and milking the cows. Back then, his grandparents used to make sausages, olive oil, cheese and wine and sell them in the weekly village market. Roberto's passion for fresh, local food took him all around the island and also to the mainland of Italy, working in different locations and gaining vast experience.

After gaining his catering degree in food management and sommelier, Roberto moved to England in 1992 and started working in Imperial Express in Darlington. He was co-owner of Sassari in Durham City as well as Middlesbrough and 12 years ago opened Café Lilli in Norton, which created the path for good food in this gem of a village.

"Helped by my wife Patricia and a great team of staff, I believe Café Lilli gives creative cooking and a lively atmosphere in an intimate, bistro-vibe café," says Roberto. "The team has vast experience of different culinary cultures. They are very passionate and innovative about food and our aim is to provide each guest with a memorable experience by only using the best quality, locally produced products to give a range of flavours to suit all tastes."

Café Lilli won Restaurant of the Year, Best Teesside and Cleveland Restaurant 2009, from The Gourmet Society. It is also a member of The Slow Food Society and use the freshest local ingredients, cooked to order, to be enjoyed around the table.

Café Lilli
Licensed Continental Cafe

PAN FRIED SCALLOPS, BUTTERNUT PUREE, POTATO TERRINE, QUAIL EGG, PICKLED RED SALSIFY, SAUCE VIERGE

SERVES 4

 Vermentino Stellato Pala
(Sardinia, Italy)

Ingredients

12 king scallops
4 quail eggs

Potato Terrine

4 large potatoes (peeled)
50g duck fat (warm)
salt and pepper

Butternut Purée

1 large butternut squash (halved, seeds removed)
70g butter
salt and pepper

Pickling Liquid And Salsify

75ml water
75ml white wine vinegar
200g sugar
½ red cabbage (sliced)
2 salsify

Sauce Vierge

1 large tomato
1 shallot (finely chopped)
2 tsp capers
1 lemon (juice of)
100ml extra virgin olive oil
1 tsp coriander seeds (crushed)
basil leaves (handful of, torn)
1 tbsp chives (chopped)

Radishes

1 black radish (thinly sliced)
1 watermelon radish (thinly sliced)

terrine mould (lined with cling film)

Method

For The Potato Terrine (Prepare the day before)
Slice the potatoes, parboil for 10 minutes, then drain. Immerse the potatoes in the duck fat and season with salt and pepper. Preheat the oven to 180°C (fan).
Layer the potato slices in the terrine and cook for 20 minutes, then press for 24 hours. To serve, cut into small dice. Serve at room temperature.

For The Butternut Purée
Preheat the oven to 180°C (fan).
Wrap the squash in foil and roast for 25 minutes or until soft. Blend until smooth in a food processor with the butter, then season with salt and pepper. Serve warm.

For The Pickling Liquid (Prepare the day before)
Bring the water, vinegar and sugar to the boil, simmer for 5 minutes. Set aside to cool. Add the red cabbage and leave overnight. Discard the cabbage.

For The Salsify
Peel the salsify quickly, then immediately put in the pickling mixture and cook for 4 minutes.
Slice and serve at room temperature.

For The Sauce Vierge
Blanch the tomato for 10 seconds, then put in cold water and peel. Discard the seeds and dice the flesh. Combine with the shallot, capers, lemon juice, olive oil, coriander seeds and herbs. Mix well.

For The Quail Eggs
Carefully place the eggs into a pan of boiling water, cook for 2½ minutes. Transfer into cold water and peel.

For The Radishes
Curl the radish into cone shapes and put in cold water.

To Serve
Pat the king scallops dry, pan fry in oil, season with salt and pepper. Swipe the purée on a large plate. Set the diced terrine along the purée and add the radishes. Place the scallops between the potato terrine, finally adding the sauce vierge and quail egg.

Chef's Tip
Work the salsify quickly so it does not oxidise. Pan fry the scallops in oil and seasoning as you put the dish together.

HERB & REGGIANO CRUSTED RACK OF LAMB

SERVES 4

🍷 *Santagostino Baglio Soria Firriato (Sicily)*

Ingredients

Rack Of Lamb

4 x 3 rack of lamb
Dijon mustard (to brush)

Herb And Reggiano Crust

4 slices dry ciabatta bread
6 sprigs parsley, 2 sprigs thyme
100g Reggiano cheese
1 sprig rosemary
20ml extra virgin olive oil
1 tsp Dijon mustard

Fondant Potato

1kg new potatoes (such as Charlotte)
2 tbsp oil, 150g butter
thyme (sprig of), 75ml chicken stock

Red Pepper Purée

8 red peppers
olive oil
2 tsp unsalted butter
½ tsp salt
freshly ground pepper

Jus

50g onion (diced), 50g celery (diced)
50g carrot (diced), 2 tsp tomato purée
500ml chicken or lamb stock

Chargrilled Vegetables

2 courgettes, 1 aubergine, 8 Chantenay carrots
8 asparagus spears, extra virgin olive oil

Pesto

wild rocket (handful of), basil (handful of)
50g roasted pine kernels (roasted)
100g Reggiano, 3 tsp extra virgin olive oil

Mint Oil

fresh mint (handful of)
50ml extra virgin olive oil

Method

For The Herb And Reggiano Crust

Place all the ingredients in a blender and blend until bright green in colour.

For The Fondant Potato

Preheat the oven to 190ºC (fan).
Cut the potatoes using an apple corer. Trim the ends with a knife to make cylinder shapes. Heat the oil in a pan and lightly cook, then add the butter, thyme and chicken stock. Roast in the oven until the stock is soaked up and the potatoes are golden brown, about 40 minutes.

For The Rack Of Lamb

Preheat the oven to 200ºC (fan).
Seal the lamb in a hot pan until golden brown. Transfer to the oven and cook for 6-7 minutes. Remove from the oven, brush with mustard, then roll the lamb in the herb crust. Return to the oven for a further 2-3 minutes. Remove the lamb and leave to rest.

Chef's Tip

Rest the lamb for as long as it has been cooked, at least 8-10 minutes.

For The Red Pepper Purée

Preheat the oven to 200ºC (fan).
Roast the peppers in the oven with a splash of olive oil for 25 minutes. Peel the skin when cool and deseed. Blitz the peppers in a blender with the butter and season to taste. Pass through a sieve to a smooth purée.

For The Jus

Sauté the onions, celery and carrot in a frying pan until softened. Add the tomato purée and stock and reduce to the desired thickness. Pass through a sieve.

For The Chargrilled Vegetables

Slice the courgettes and aubergine lengthways, using a knife to make into long ribbons. *Blanch* the carrots and asparagus in salted, boiling water for 4-5 minutes, then drain. Heat a griddle pan with extra virgin olive oil and chargrill all the vegetables.

For The Pesto

Place all the ingredients in a blender and blitz until well mixed.

For The Mint Oil

Blitz the mint leaves in a blender with the oil. Drain through a sieve.

To Serve

Serve as pictured.

CHOCOLATE ORANGE SORBET TART

SERVES 8

 L'Ecru Passito Bianco, Sicily (Italy) or
Temptation Beer, Durham Brewery (UK)

Ingredients

Shortcrust Pastry Case
125g plain flour
salt (pinch of)
55g butter (cubed)
45ml iced water

Tart Filling
240ml double cream
2 oranges (zest of)
400g sweet milk chocolate (broken up)

Blood Orange Sorbet
250g blood orange flesh
150g sugar
250ml water

Dark Chocolate Parfait
100g 70% (minimum) dark chocolate (melted)
4 egg yolks
60g caster sugar
400ml double cream (whipped to soft peak)

Orange Jelly
75ml water
75ml fresh orange juice (no bits)
40g caster sugar
1 sheet gelatine (soaked)

Salted Caramel
50ml double cream
60g dark brown sugar
½ tsp vanilla extract
salt flakes (pinch of)

Toffee Macadamia Nuts
75g caster sugar, 60ml water
16 macadamia nuts, 16 toothpicks

Chocolate Soil
6 Oreo cookies or dark chocolate biscuits (blitzed
to a soil texture)

Garnish
edible flowers, mint (sprigs of), cocoa (to dust)

20cm tart case

Method

For The Shortcrust Pastry Case
Preheat the oven to 180°C (fan).
Pulse the flour, salt and butter into a food processor 4-5 times.
Add the water, a little at a time, until the pastry comes together.
Wrap in cling film and place in the fridge for 30 minutes.
Roll the chilled pastry to ½cm thick on a clean surface dusted
with a little flour. Carefully transfer the pastry to the tart case.
Blind bake for 12-15 minutes, then leave to cool.

> **Chef's Tip**
> Use a small ball of excess pastry to push the pastry into the
> tart case. Leave the excess pastry over the sides of the tart
> case and tidy up with a serrated knife after it has been baked.
> Prepare all elements of this dish in advance.

For The Tart Filling
Bring the cream and zest to the boil.
Put the chocolate in a bowl and slowly add the hot cream
mixture, stirring at all times. When smooth and glossy, pour into
the tart case. Set in the fridge for 7-8 hours, or overnight.

For The Blood Orange Sorbet
Pass the flesh through a sieve to remove any bits. Bring the
sugar and water to the boil, then stir in the smooth pulp.
Remove from the heat and pour into a plastic freezer container.
Freeze, stirring the mixture every 1-2 hours. Repeat 3 or 4 times,
then leave to freeze.

For The Dark Chocolate Parfait
Mix the yolks and caster sugar until light and fluffy and tripled
in size. Mix the melted chocolate in, a little at a time. Whisk the
cream into the chocolate mixture. Place into moulds or suitable
container and freeze.

For The Orange Jelly
Bring the water, orange juice and sugar to the boil. Stir in the
gelatine until melted. Set in a suitable container in the fridge.

For The Salted Caramel
Gently whisk the cream, sugar and vanilla over a low heat. Bring
to the boil, simmer for 2 minutes, add the salt and leave to cool.

For The Toffee Macadamia Nuts
Heat the caster sugar and water to 155°C. Secure the nuts on
the toothpicks and carefully dip into the caramel. Leave to drip
and harden.

To Serve
Drizzle the plates with caramel. Lay a thin layer of jelly on the
plates and top with the parfait and a *quenelle* of sorbet.
Place the tart alongside. Adorn with the nuts and soil, dust with
cocoa and garnish as pictured.

088
CHEZ MAL BAR & BRASSERIE

Malmaison, Quayside, Newcastle upon Tyne, NE1 3DX

0191 3898 627
www.malmaison.com/newcastle Twitter: @TheNewcastleMal

A blink away from the winking eye of the Millennium Bridge in the city's bustling Quayside, Malmaison Newcastle is the perfect destination to stay, meet, drink or eat. Forget everything you ever believed about hotel dining and bars. Start believing in simple British classic dishes, uncompromising in quality and very generous in portion. Believe in a glittering choice of superstar wines and Champagnes. Believe in the cheeky one after work, the school night mojito, that world famous fromage with a refreshing white Rioja just for the hell of it. Following an investment programme that has seen upgrades to all areas of the business, Malmaison Newcastle unveils its centrepiece, Chez Mal Brasserie and Bar. For those that graced the hotel in its first incarnation in 1997, they will note a return to the original format with the stylish new Chez Mal Brasserie once again overlooking the River Tyne and its iconic Millennium Bridge and The Baltic, standing in eyesight out of the picture, arched windows. With a brighter, fresher look, the brasserie has shed its dark wood and black leather in favour of a more vibrant colour palette.

Exposed, distressed brick walls bedecked in quirky pop art takes on classic French portraits of the original Château de Malmaison occupants Napoleon and Josephine. By day the picture windows bathe the brasserie in light. Come dusk into night the atmosphere is classic moody Malmaison. All bedrooms have undergone a stylish refurbishment with great beds for sleepy heads, power showers, flatscreen TVs, serious wines and naughty nibbles. Other luxuries include take home toiletries and 'vroom' room service for breakfast, dinner or midnight munchies.

"We have a young, passionate team in the kitchen and all strive for excellence in our food. Because we are a small kitchen, everything from our ice creams to terrines really is a team effort!" Sandeep Singh, head chef.

AHI TUNA TARTARE, PICKLED GINGER, WASABI, AVOCADO & SOY DRESSING

SERVES 4

Kung Fu Girl Riesling 2013, Charles Smith
(Washington State, USA)

Ingredients

Ahi Tuna Tartare

320g yellow fin tuna
olive oil
sea salt
1 lime (juice of)

Avocado Dice

1½ ripe avocados
1 lime (juice of)

Avocado And Wasabi Purée

½ ripe avocado
½ lime (juice of)
wasabi paste (to taste)

Soy Dressing

3 tbsp light soy sauce
2 tbsp mirin
1 tbsp Dijon mustard
1 tbsp rice wine vinegar
1 tbsp honey
2 tbsp kecap manis

Homemade Pickled Ginger

1 thumb ginger (peeled)
3 tbsp caster sugar
1 tsp rice wine vinegar
2 tbsp white wine vinegar

Garnish

Thai basil cress
black sesame seeds (toasted)

4 x 5cm square moulds

Method

For The Tuna Tartare

Dice the tuna into 3mm squares. Dress with extra virgin olive oil and sea salt.

> **Chef's Tip**
> Use fresh lime juice to enhance the flavour of yellow fin tuna.

For The Avocado Dice

Place half an avocado into a bowl and mash with a fork. Spritz over the lime juice. Dice the remaining avocado and add to the bowl. Season and mix well. Divide between the moulds and flatten. Cover with greaseproof paper until needed.

For The Avocado And Wasabi Purée

Blend the avocado, lime juice and wasabi until smooth.

For The Soy Dressing

Reduce the ingredients almost by half until thick.

For The Homemade Pickled Ginger

Heat the vinegars and sugar until dissolved. Finely slice the ginger using a potato peeler then add to the liquid. Set aside.

To Serve

Place the tuna on top of the avocado base and sprinkle with toasted sesame seeds. Pipe or *quenelle* a small amount of the purée onto the plate and top with Thai basil cress. Finish with the pickled ginger and soy dressing.

NY STRIP STEAK, BEARNAISE SAUCE, SPINACH GRATIN, TRUFFLE MASH

SERVES 4

Emiliana Coyam 2011 Organic, Colchagua Valley (Chile)

Ingredients

Steaks

4 x 350g NY strip steaks
olive oil
butter (large knob of)
Maldon salt and pepper (to season)

Béarnaise Sauce

100ml white wine vinegar
1 tbsp white wine
5 stalks tarragon
1 shallot (diced)
4 white peppercorns
2 egg yolks
250g unsalted butter (melted)
2 tbsp tarragon and chervil (chopped)

Truffle Mash

4 red Rooster potatoes
2 tbsp crème fraîche
truffle oil (drizzle of)
seasoning
100g Westcombe cheddar (grated)
chives (chopped, to garnish)
sea salt (to garnish)

Spinach Gratin

200g spinach
60ml béchamel sauce (to bind)
50g Gruyère cheese (grated)
1 clove garlic (chopped)
butter (knob of)
seasoning
truffle oil (drizzle of)
30g breadcrumbs
30g Parmesan cheese

Garnish

4 *confit* beef tomatoes
watercress

Method

For The Béarnaise Sauce

Over a gentle heat, infuse the vinegar and wine with the shallot, tarragon and peppercorns.

Place the yolks in a mixing bowl over a *bain-marie*. Pass the vinegar through a sieve and add to the egg yolks. Whisk to a *sabayon* until doubled in volume.

Gradually add the melted butter until *emulsified*. Season to taste. Add the chopped herbs to finish.

For The Truffle Mash

Preheat the oven to 190ºC.

Bake the potatoes until soft. Scoop out the flesh and pass twice through a drum sieve whilst still hot. Mix in the crème fraîche, truffle oil, seasoning and Westcombe cheddar.

Check the consistency, adding more crème fraîche if required. You should be able to taste the truffle and cheese. Pipe into a brûlée dish; it must fit up to the edges. Bake for 15 minutes until hot. Finish under the grill. Garnish with sea salt, truffle oil and chives.

For The Spinach Gratin

Preheat the oven to 190ºC.

Blanch the spinach in boiling, salted water, then place in iced water. Squeeze dry and chop.

Fry the garlic in the butter for 1-2 minutes. Add the spinach and béchamel sauce to bind, then stir in the Gruyère, seasoning well with salt and pepper and the truffle oil. Place into an ovenproof dish, smooth the top, then sprinkle over the breadcrumbs and Parmesan. Bake for 20 minutes until hot. Finish under the grill.

For The Steaks

Rub the steaks with olive oil and season on both sides.

Place the steaks in a hot pan or *plancha*. Cook on both sides to just under your desired cooking preference. Add a large knob of butter and foam over the steaks, turning occasionally.

Pass the butter through a sieve into a small bowl and keep warm.

Allow the steaks to rest, then flash under a hot grill just before serving. Slice the steaks on a slight angle, season and fan out on the plate.

Chef's Tip

This cut of steak is best served medium rare.

To Serve

Spoon the cooking butter over the steaks and serve as pictured. Garnish with watercress and *confit* beef tomatoes.

MALMAISON HOT CHOCOLATE

SERVES 4

🍷 *Els Pyreneus Maury Grenat 2012,*
Languedoc-Roussillon (France)

Ingredients

Marshmallows

450g sugar
200ml water
9 sheets gelatine (softened in cold water)
2 large egg whites
1 tsp vanilla extract
1 tbsp liquid glucose
50/50 icing sugar and cornflour (to dust)

Crème Chantilly

142ml double cream
2 tbsp icing sugar
vanilla extract (few drops of)

Valrhona Chocolate Sauce

250ml double cream
50g liquid glucose
150g Valrhona dark chocolate (chopped)

To Serve

4 balls white chocolate ice cream
4 balls vanilla ice cream

4 coffee cups and saucers

Method

For The Marshmallows

Boil the sugar and water to 127ºC, stir in the gelatine. Beat the egg whites to stiff peaks. Pour the sugar liquid onto the eggs with the vanilla and slowly beat for 10 minutes until thick. Pour onto a non-stick tray and leave to cool. Cut into bite-sized pieces, then roll in the cornflour mix.

For The Crème Chantilly

Whisk the cream with the sugar and vanilla extract to a stiff peak.

For The Valrhona Chocolate Sauce

Gently heat the cream and the glucose. Add the chocolate and stir until melted and fully incorporated.

> **Chef's Tip**
> Use a bitter dark chocolate for the chocolate sauce to help balance the sweetness of the crème Chantilly and white chocolate ice cream.

To Serve

Place a ball of each ice cream in the coffee cups. Pipe a swirl of crème Chantilly onto the ice cream and place the marshmallows on top.

Serve the warm chocolate sauce in a jug and allow your guests to pour it over at the table.

098
DCH RESTAURANT

Dean Court Hotel, Duncombe Place, York, YO1 7EF

01904 625 082
www.deancourt-york.co.uk Twitter: @DeanCourtYork

The Best Western Plus Dean Court Hotel was originally built in 1865 as three separate dwellings, housing Clergy of the Minster, and is situated on the corner of Petergate, the main Roman road that ran through the city of York. The hotel has a rare sign on the side elevation - a set of crossed keys. These represent the keys to heaven given to St Peter, endorsing the original building's association to the Minster. After the end of World War I the Thwaites family bought the middle section and accepted paying guests.

The 37-bedroom hotel, many of the rooms with magnificent views of York Minster, has gained 4 star status, a 2 AA Rosette restaurant, an all day Court Café Bar and two small function rooms.

Head chef Benji Thornton, a local man born in York 31 years ago, has lived and worked in hotels and restaurants for the past 14 years after completing his training. His passion is cooking, especially with Yorkshire ingredients, foraged and local, which is reflected in his menus. When creating a dish - especially game, he uses all the component parts. Trying new dishes, always thinking local and seasonal, he checks the origin of ingredients and by motivating, developing and coaching his team, shares his dedication to the industry.

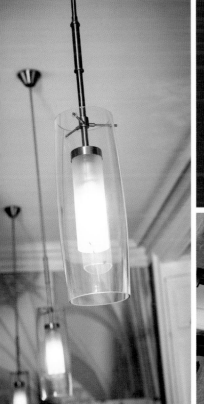

Enjoy an unrivalled and spectacular setting in this 2 AA Rosette restaurant. The creative menu draws inspiration from local produce and is skillfully executed to offer a unique dining experience.

SMOKED DUCK BREAST PASTRAMI, SALT BAKED BABY BEETROOT, PICKLED BLACKBERRIES, SEED TUILE

SERVES 4

 Pinot Noir Kura, Martinborough (New Zealand)

Ingredients

Smoked Duck Breast Pastrami

2 duck breasts (skin on)

Cure

1 tbsp course grain salt
1 tsp ground black pepper
1 tsp ground coriander
1 tsp dark brown sugar
½ tsp ground juniper berries
½ tsp pink salt
¼ tsp ground ginger
¼ tsp garlic powder
¼ tsp ground cloves

Rub

1½ tbsp black pepper (coarsely ground)
2 tsp coriander seed (coarsely ground)
1 tsp juniper berries (coarsely ground)
¼ tsp garlic powder
2 handfuls light smoking wood (apple or cherry)

Salt Baked Baby Beetroot

2 candy beetroots
4 baby beetroots
2 golden beetroot
50g salt

Pickled Blackberries

½ punnet blackberries
100ml water
100ml white wine
100g sugar

Seed Tuile

75g unsalted butter
75g sugar, 25g glucose
25ml milk
150g sesame seeds

Method

For The Smoked Duck Breast Pastrami

For The Cure (Prepare 72 hours ahead)

Combine all the ingredients. Coat the duck breasts entirely and place in a large, re-sealable plastic bag. Place in the fridge and cure for 72 hours, flipping the bag twice a day.

For The Rub

Remove the duck breasts from the bag and wash off as much cure as possible under cold, running water. Place the breasts in a large container and fill with water. Soak for 2 hours, replacing the water every 30 minutes. Remove from the water and pat dry.

Combine the rub ingredients in a small bowl and coat the breasts in the rub mix.

Fire up the smoker or grill to 107°C, adding wood chunks once at the temperature. When the wood is smoking, place the duck breasts in, skin-side down, and smoke for 1½-2 hours until the centre of the breast reaches 74°C.

> **Chef's Tip**
>
> If you don't have a smoker, you can use a heavy bottomed pan with a wire rack placed inside, or a deep flat tray for smoking the duck. You can use a variety of different woods for smoking; apple or cherry get the best flavours.

For The Salt Baked Baby Beetroot

Preheat the oven to 160°C.

Place the different beetroot on separate sheets of foil to stop the colours combining. Add the salt to the parcels and close the foil. Bake for 40 minutes.

For The Pickled Blackberries

Bring the water, white wine and sugar to the boil. Remove from heat and, once cool, add the blackberries.

For The Seed Tuile

Preheat the oven to 160°C.

Bring the butter, sugar, glucose and milk to the boil in a pan. Add the seeds once the sugar has dissolved. Spread onto parchment paper and cook in the oven for 10 minutes.

To Serve

Serve as pictured.

PAN FRIED PARTRIDGE BREAST, WILD MUSHROOM & CONFIT LEG BONBON, SWEETCORN PUREE, PARTRIDGE JUS

SERVES 4

 Duca di Sasseta Chianti, Barbanera, Tuscany (Italy)

Ingredients

8 partridge breasts

Wild Mushroom And Confit Leg Bonbons

8 pigeon legs
duck fat (to cover)
2 tbsp brandy
1 chicken breast, 1 egg white
150ml double cream
100g mixed wild mushrooms
2 small shallots, 2 cloves garlic
30g butter, breadcrumbs (to *pane*)

Partridge Jus

1 carrot (finely chopped)
1 white onion (chopped)
1 stick celery (chopped)
1 clove garlic (crushed)
100ml white wine vinegar
3 sprigs thyme, 6 juniper berries
10 coriander seeds, 8 white peppercorns
partridge bones and trimmings (roasted)
1 litre good game stock

Potato Rösti

1 onion (chopped)
50g butter
1 clove garlic (crushed)
1 sprig thyme (picked)
2 large potatoes
2 eggs
salt

Sweetcorn Purée

250g sweetcorn kernels, 150ml double cream
salt (to season), 100ml full-fat milk

Vegetables

8 baby corn
8 spears tender stem broccoli

Method

For The Wild Mushroom And Confit Leg Bonbons

Preheat the oven to 150°C.

Cover the legs with duck fat and roast for 3 hours until tender. Pick the meat from the legs, reserve the bones.

Blend the remaining ingredients (less the breadcrumbs) in a processor to make a chicken mousse and season well. Bind the picked meat with the chicken mousse. Roll into 4 balls, then stick in a bone. *Pane* the bonbons in the breadcrumbs, then fry in a pan. Finish off in the oven (160°C) for 6-8 minutes.

For The Partridge Breasts

Heat a little olive oil in a pan. When hot, fry the breasts for 1-2 minutes on each side. Remove from the pan and set aside somewhere warm.

For The Partridge Jus

Sauté the vegetables and spices in a hot pan, caramelise but don't burn. Add the vinegar and reduce to a syrup. Add the carcasses and the stock to the pan, reduce by half. Pass the jus through a sieve, then return to the pan and reduce to a syrup consistency. Check seasoning and remove from heat.

> **Chef's Tip**
> To get the best results for the partridge jus, simmer on the stove for a few hours. Roasting the carcasses well gets the best flavour out of them. Once made, whisk in a little butter to the jus to give a clean and more intense flavour.

For The Potato Rösti

Cook the onion in a little butter, add the garlic and thyme and cook for a further 2 minutes. Allow to cool. Grate the potato and season, add the cooled onion and eggs and mix in well. When ready to use, cook in a flat pan with a little oil and butter. Allow to crisp before turning over and cooking on the other side.

For The Sweetcorn Purée

Bring all the ingredients to a simmer in a saucepan. When the corn is tender, remove from the heat and blend until smooth. Season to taste and pass through a fine sieve.

For The Vegetables

Blanch in boiling salted water for 3-4 minutes, then char on a hot griddle.

To Serve

Serve as pictured.

APPLE CRUMBLE

SERVES 4

 Gewurztraminer Pfaffenheim, Alsace (France)

Ingredients

Caramelised Apples

2 apples (peeled, cored and cut into desired shapes)
100g butter
125g brown sugar

Apple Crisp

1 apple (finely sliced)
200ml water
200g granulated sugar
75g icing sugar

Burnt Butter Ice Cream

250g unsalted butter
220g brown sugar
½ tsp salt
8 egg yolks
1 tbsp vanilla extract
725ml double cream
120ml full-fat milk

Crumble

50g oats
40g wholemeal flour
15g wheat germ
50g walnuts (roughly chopped)
salt (pinch of)
50g caster sugar
1 tsp ground cinnamon
½ tsp ground ginger
½ nutmeg (freshly grated)
60g unsalted butter

Cinnamon And Aniseed Foam

250ml double cream
100ml full-fat milk
1 stick cinnamon
2 star anise
1 leaf gelatine (softened)
canister with 2 gas bulbs

Method

For The Apple Crisp (Prepare the day before)

Boil the water and sugar to create a syrup. Coat the apple slices in the syrup and icing sugar and leave in an oven (80ºC) overnight.

For The Burnt Butter Ice Cream

Melt the butter in a small saucepan over a medium heat. Cook, swirling the pan occasionally, until the butter turns a deep golden colour and you see dark flecks. Transfer to a bowl and allow to cool until no longer warm to the touch, about 20 minutes. Cream together the browned butter, sugar and salt until light and fluffy. Whisk in the yolks and vanilla extract until combined. Slowly pour in the cream and milk, whisking the entire time, until there are no lumps. Transfer the mixture to a large saucepan over a medium high heat and bring to the boil, stirring occasionally. Simmer, stirring as needed, until thickened and it can coat the back of a spoon. Chill, then churn in an ice cream machine.

For The Crumble

Place everything in a pan and mix together over a low heat until the ingredients have soaked up the butter.

For The Cinnamon And Aniseed Foam

Gently heat the cream and milk in a pan. Toast the cinnamon and star anise in a separate pan, then add to the milk mix and allow to infuse. Strain the mix, then return to the heat and add the gelatine. Leave at room temperature for 1 hour. Pass through a sieve and into the charged canister.

Chef's Tip

Instead of using a creamer for the foam, you can add a teaspoon of lecithin and use a hand blender to create foam.

For The Caramelised Apples

Melt the butter and sugar in a pan. Add the apples and cook until tender. Serve warm.

To Serve

Serve as pictured.

FEVERSHAM ARMS HOTEL

High Street, Helmsley, North Yorkshire, YO62 5AG

01439 770 766
www.fevershamarmshotel.com Twitter: @fevershamarms

The Feversham Arms Hotel & Verbena Spa is a secluded luxury retreat, nestled in the picturesque market town of Helmsley in North Yorkshire. Your dining experience at the Feversham Arms starts from the moment you arrive. Choose a squashy sofa, either nestled in a corner or next to a real fire, and take your time to consider the three menus.

The Signature Tasting Menu includes six courses of deeply flavoursome dishes. The Seasonal Market Menu changes regularly and uses the best local produce that ties in with the seasons. Head chef Norman Mackenzie is a keen forager and this menu reflects what might have been found in the vast countryside surrounding the hotel on any given day. The à la carte menu gives guests the freedom to choose from a wide selection of dishes, from light vegetarian or fish options to the 'Bloody Good Cuts of Meat' section, from which many items are carved at the table.

From the lounges, guests may move through to dine in the air-lit restaurant or cosy snug, both of which offer a relaxed setting with a convivial buzz of people enjoying themselves.

"We don't want you to feel that you can't speak above a whisper; this is your time to catch-up with friends, colleagues or loved ones and we want you to feel as comfortable as possible," says Norman.

Located on the River Rye and surrounded by the stunning countryside of the North York Moors National Park, the hotel and restaurant's secluded location is the perfect hideaway.

BEEF CARPACCIO 'PASTURE FLAVOURS', NETTLES, PICKLED THISTLE & SHALLOTS SOAKED IN HOWARDIAN GOLD BEER

SERVES 4

 Howardian Gold Ale from Helmsley Brewery (UK)

Ingredients

Beef Carpaccio

400g centre cut fillet Dexter beef
1 tbsp espelette (basque) pepper
1 tsp sel rose
1 tbsp oil
200g black mustard leaf (chopped)

Beer Soaked Shallots

1 shallot (peeled, sliced into ½cm rings)
100ml Howardian Gold beer

Nettle Fluid Gel

450ml vegetable stock
2 handfuls young nettle tops
2 leaves gelatine (soaked)

Pickled Thistle

500ml Champagne vinegar
1 litre water
105g white sugar
30g salt
15g yellow mustard seeds
1 clove
1 star anise
12 thistle heads (peeled, choke removed)

Garnish

100g wood sorrel

Method

For The Beef Carpaccio

Trim any excess fat and sinew from the fillet. Roll in the espelette pepper, then leave to marinate in the fridge for 1 hour. Remove from the fridge and season with the sel rose.

Place a frying pan on a high heat, add the oil and seal the fillet until golden brown all over.

Remove from the pan and roll in the mustard leaf. Wrap tightly in cling film and place in the fridge.

For The Beer Soaked Shallots

Soak the larger outer rings in the beer for 1 hour. Discard the small, central rings.

For The Nettle Fluid Gel

Bring the stock to the boil, add the young nettle tops and blend. Pass through muslin and season.

Add the gelatine to the warm stock and once dissolved, place in the fridge to set for 2-3 hours. Once set, blitz in a blender until it reaches the consistency of a smooth fluid gel.

For The Pickled Thistle (Prepare in advance)

Bring all the ingredients, except the thistle heads, to the boil in a saucepan. Remove from the heat and leave to infuse for 12 hours. Strain through a muslin cloth and store in a glass bottle to use as and when required. (Makes more than required).

Thinly slice the thistle heads and soak in 200ml of the pickling liquor until ready to serve.

To Serve

Thinly slice the fillet to make the carpaccio, then place in a line on the plate.

Dot the nettle fluid gel around the plate. Scatter the wood sorrel on top of the beef. Finish by placing the drained shallot rings and thistle on top.

> **Chef's Tip**
>
> All elements of this dish can be made a few days in advance and saved until you are ready to eat it. The dish has a great impact, but takes just minutes to plate up and serve!

FORAGED LOBSTER SALAD

SERVES 4

 *Pol Roger Rosé Champagne 2004
(France)*

Ingredients

Lobster Salad

2 lobsters (head and claws removed)
500g butter
8 raw king prawns (peeled, vein removed)
20ml lemon oil
12 needle leeks
20ml truffle vinaigrette
4g samphire
2 breakfast radish (thinly sliced)
1 pickled globe artichoke (*julienne*)
100g fresh peas
100g broad beans

Croutons

2 slices wholemeal bread (crusts removed)
1g poppy seeds
salt (pinch of)

Foraged Herbs And Flowers

land cress, watercress
didanter, sweet cicely
wild fennel, water celery
wood sorrel, golden saxifrage
camomile leaves
ox eye daisy leaves
nasturtium, robert flower
pennywort
young dandelion leaf
raspberry leaf
purslane
stonecrop
wild pea flower
ramson seeds
mallow flowers
sea purslane

To Serve

Wharfe Valley oil (drizzle of)
20ml smoked roe *emulsion*
10g summer truffle (thinly sliced)

Method

For The Lobster Salad

Clarify and bring the butter to 50°C. Place the lobster in the butter for 45 minutes.

Marinate the prawns in the lemon oil for 1 hour.

Blanch the needle leeks and refresh in cold water, dry thoroughly, then place in the truffle vinaigrette.

Blanch and refresh the samphire.

For The Croutons

Preheat the oven to 120°C (fan).

Roll out the bread with a rolling pin, brush with the *clarified butter* from the lobster, then sprinkle with poppy seeds and salt. Cut into circles (roughly 1½ cm in diameter). Bake for 8 minutes.

For The Foraged Herbs And Flowers

Thoroughly wash and dry all the foraged herbs and flowers.

To Assemble And Serve

Mix all the foraged salad ingredients, radish and artichoke in a large bowl. Drizzle with the Wharfe Valley oil, then divide evenly between the four plates.

Warm the peas, broad beans and samphire in a little butter in a shallow frying pan, then gently add the needle leeks. Share this evenly between the four plates.

Cut the lobster tails in half and remove the flesh from the shell. Arrange on top of the salad and vegetables.

Place the prawns onto a metal plate and cook with a blowtorch for roughly 30 seconds until cooked through, then add 2 prawns to each plate. Dot the smoked roe *emulsion* around the plate to dress. Scatter with croutons.

> **Chef's Tip**
> If you don't have a chef's blowtorch, skewer your prawns and cook on a gas hob. This method of cooking prawns is great as they cook quickly but retain their juiciness.

ROSE PANNA COTTA, ELDERFLOWER GRANITA, SORBET

SERVES 4

 Moscato d'Asti 2013, Vietti (Italy)

Ingredients

Rose Panna Cotta

140ml full-fat milk
15g caster sugar
dried rose petals (pinch of)
15ml rose water
2 leaves gelatine (soaked)
100ml double cream

Elderflower Granita

400g sugar
1 litre water
2 large handfuls elderflowers

Elderflower Sorbet

900g sugar
1½ litres water
250g glucose
2 large handfuls elderflowers

To Dress

fresh rose petals
crystallised rose petals (crushed)

4 glasses

Method

For The Rose Panna Cotta

Add the milk, sugar, rose petals and rose water to a saucepan, bring to the boil, then take off the heat.

Stir in the gelatine and, once dissolved, strain the milk mixture onto the cream and stir.

Pour into a glass (we do this at an angle for effect) and leave to set in the fridge for 3-4 hours.

For The Elderflower Granita

Bring the sugar and water to the boil. Simmer for a couple of minutes, then add the elderflowers.

Take off the heat and leave to infuse for 1 hour. Strain through muslin and chill.

Once cold, pour into a shallow tray and place in the freezer.

Stir with a fork every hour until set, the result will look like crushed ice.

For The Elderflower Sorbet

Bring the sugar, water and glucose to the boil. Simmer for a couple of minutes, then add the elderflowers.

Take off the heat and leave to infuse for about 1 hour. Strain through muslin and chill.

Once cool, churn in an ice cream machine.

To Serve

Spoon the granita onto the panna cotta. Using an ice cream scoop, place a ball of sorbet on the top. Dress the dish with fresh rose petals and crushed, crystallised rose petals.

> **Chef's Tip**
>
> Dog rose petals are best for this recipe as they are very fragrant and full of flavour.

118
HEADLAM HALL
COUNTRY HOTEL & SPA

Headlam, Near Gainford, Darlington, DL2 3HA

01325 730 238
www.headlamhall.co.uk Twitter: @Headlamhall Facebook: Headlam Hall

Headlam Hall is a charming Jacobean country house in rural Teesdale, standing in fabulous walled gardens and surrounded by its own rolling farmland. This family owned and run hotel has built its reputation around great food, friendly service and genuine hospitality. As well as owning Headlam Hall, the Robinson family also farms the surrounding land, so has a good understanding of the importance of local produce and developing strong relationships with quality suppliers.

The hall itself dates back to the mid-17th Century and there is plenty to remind you of its rich history, with the interiors combining stunning period features and antique furnishings, with sympathetic contemporary touches to provide comfort and elegance.

Food can be enjoyed in both the bar area and the stylish orangery which looks out onto a secluded, walled terrace. There is also good scope for private dining and the beautiful Georgian-styled drawing room opens onto a stepped terrace overlooking the immaculate main lawns. You can enjoy a pre-dinner drink by the fire in the bar and after dinner coffee and liqueurs in the impressive main hall lounge that features stone pillars and the original carved oak fireplace.

The four acres of walled gardens are a real feature of this country house with colourful herbaceous borders, an ornamental canal and a productive kitchen garden amidst the ancient beech hedges. The hotel also offers 38 bedrooms, an award-winning spa and a challenging 9 hole golf course.

The kitchen team, led by Derek Thomson, creates its menus with seasonality and to reflect this rural region. The Hall gardens also provide home-grown vegetables, fruits and herbs for the Headlam larder.

PAN SEARED SCALLOPS, PARSNIP PUREE, CHORIZO SAUSAGE, BLACK PUDDING & HERB OIL

SERVES 4

Azumbre Verdejo
(Spain)

Ingredients

Scallops

12 medium scallops
Maldon sea salt
oil (for frying)
10g butter
½ lemon (juice of)

Parsnip Purée

4 parsnips (peeled, quartered, cored)
300ml full-fat milk
25g butter
salt
white pepper

Herb Oil

100g parsley
100g rocket
100g watercress
100g sage
200ml olive oil

Garnish

75g chorizo (sliced)
75g black pudding (1cm dice)
4 rashers streaky bacon
micro herbs

Method

For The Parsnip Purée

Roughly chop the parsnips and simmer in the milk for about 30 minutes until soft. Drain, reserving the liquid. Blend the parsnips and butter in a blender until smooth, adding a little of the reserved cooking liquid if required. Season to taste and pass through a fine sieve. Keep warm.

For The Herb Oil

Blitz all the ingredients in a food processor until the oil is green. Pass through a fine sieve and set aside.

For The Scallops

Season the scallops. Heat a little oil in a large frying pan and sear the scallops for 2 minutes, flip over and cook for a further minute. Add the butter and a squeeze of lemon. Remove from the pan and keep warm.

> **Chef's Tip**
>
> For presentation, seal the scallops on the smooth side first to get colour and serve with that side up.

To Finish

Pan fry the chorizo, black pudding and bacon until lightly coloured. Place on kitchen roll to soak up any excess oil.

To Plate

Start by swiping the purée down the centre of the plates. Arrange 3 scallops around the purée and place the chorizo and black pudding around the plate. Drizzle over some herb oil and finish with micro herbs.

PAN SEARED VENISON LOIN, SAVOY CABBAGE, THYME FONDANT POTATO, DURHAM GIN & JUNIPER BERRY JUS

SERVES 4

 Deakin Estate Shiraz
(Australia)

Ingredients

Venison Loin

1 venison loin (trimmed, portioned into 4)
Maldon sea salt
cracked black pepper
50ml olive oil
1 sprig thyme
70g butter

Fondant Potato

200g butter
2 cloves garlic (peeled, lightly crushed)
4 sprigs thyme
4 potatoes (peeled, squared)
100ml chicken stock

Juniper And Gin Jus

30g juniper berries
75ml Durham gin (or a good quality gin)
250ml venison or veal stock
salt
pepper

Savoy Cabbage

150ml vegetable stock
40g butter
½ Savoy cabbage
20g roasted chestnuts
salt
pepper

Garnish

100g pancetta lardons

Method

For The Venison Loin

Preheat the oven to 180ºC (fan).

Season the venison with sea salt and cracked pepper. Place in a large pan on a high heat with the thyme and olive oil, turning regularly until coloured all the way round. Add the butter and place in the oven for about 5 minutes. Remove from the oven and rest for 10 minutes to ensure the meat is tender.

For The Fondant Potatoes

Melt the butter with the garlic and thyme in a frying pan over a medium heat. Add the potatoes and fry until golden, turn and fry on the other side. Pour in the stock and simmer on a low heat until tender. Carefully remove and keep warm.

Chef's Tip

To help keep the fondant potato from sticking, season the pan with a sprinkle of salt before placing the potatoes in.

For The Juniper And Gin Jus

Add the juniper berries and gin to a hot pan (being careful as it will set alight). Cook out until the flames start to die out. Add the stock and reduce until you get the consistency you require. Season and pass through a sieve. Keep warm.

For The Savoy Cabbage

Bring the stock and butter to the boil in a pan. Add the cabbage and cook until most of the liquid has reduced. Mix in the chestnuts and season.

For The Garnish

Fry the pancetta lardons in a little oil until crispy. Place on kitchen roll to soak any excess fat.

To Serve

Place a fondant potato and a little cabbage in the centre of the plate. Slice each venison portion into 3 pieces and lay over the cabbage. Sprinkle over the crispy pancetta, then spoon over the jus and serve.

BLACK FOREST PLATTER

SERVES 4

 Campbell's Rutherglen Muscat (Australia)

Ingredients

Chocolate Cake

3 medium eggs
75g sugar
50g honey
50g ground almonds
75g self-raising flour (sifted)
14g cocoa powder (sifted)
80ml double cream
37g dark chocolate (melted)
65g butter (melted)
35ml rum

Cherry Panna Cotta

285ml full-fat milk
285ml double cream
85g caster sugar
3 leaves gelatine (soaked)
150ml cherry purée

Cherry Sorbet

300ml sugar syrup
300ml cherry purée

Garnish

cherries soaked in kirsch
cherry purée

26cm x 18cm cake tin (lined, greased)

Method

For The Chocolate Cake

Preheat the oven to 150°C (fan).

Whisk the eggs, sugar and honey together. Stir in the almonds and dry ingredients then add the cream. Incorporate the melted chocolate and butter. Add the rum and mix well. Bake in the prepared tin for 30 minutes.

For The Cherry Panna Cotta

Bring the milk, cream and sugar to the boil. Stir in the gelatine until dissolved. Whisk in the cherry purée, pass through a fine sieve and set in a non-stick tray.

For The Cherry Sorbet

Mix the ingredients together and place in the freezer. Whisk every 30 minutes to break up the ice crystals. Repeat until fully frozen and smooth.

Chef's Tip

Before serving, brush some kirsch or rum over the chocolate to give the dessert more of a Black Forest gâteau taste.

To Serve

Slice a piece of the cake and place just off centre of the plate. Using a round cutter, cut out a piece of the panna cotta and place next to the cake. Add a nice scoop of the sorbet overlapping the sponge. Garnish with cherries and the cherry purée.

128
THE HERB GARDEN

Arch 8 Westgate Road, Newcastle, Tyne and Wear, NE1 1SA

0191 222 0491
www.theherbgardenuk.com Twitter: @theherbgardenuk

The Herb Garden opened its doors in November 2013 - and soon established itself as one of Newcastle's most exciting pizza restaurant. Situated inside a railway arch in the heart of the city, the founders have built a unique industrial-meets-nature dining experience.

Visit The Herb Garden and you'll find yourself in an otherworldly setting. Sit amid the hydroponic glow of the walled herb garden, beneath a sky of lanterns, and choose from a menu sourced from vegetables that quite literally grow around you.

This is the vision of restaurateur and designer Richard Marks, set builder Ryan Darrington and of Lucy Clinch, former private chef aboard one of the world's most luxurious super yachts. Together they have created a place where diners can enjoy freshly grown, exotic ingredients at affordable prices in a relaxed setting - there's a strict no booking policy at The Herb Garden.

All produce is cooked using wood-fired pizza ovens and the sous-vide method more commonly found in Michelin starred restaurants (you won't find a fryer or hob here). While the inventive pizza menu is a complete departure from your standard Hawaiian fare, expect toppings like broccoli, pecorino, walnut and thyme, and signature salads like the 'Flower Power' with chicken, sweet potato, feta and edible flowers. The Herb Garden naturally prides itself in all that it grows, however it also pays particular attention to sourcing the best quality meats to complement its produce.

Of course, underpinning all this is the founders' vision - to serve only the freshest ingredients in a fantastic herb garden setting.

There's nothing 'normal' about The Herb Garden, from its living wall of salads to Herby, the giant roller skating horse that greets you at the door. Come and have your senses blown.

'SOUPER' HOLY GUACAMOLE

SERVES 4

🍷 *Geyser Peak Sauvignon Blanc, California (USA)*

Method

For The 'Souper' Holy Guacamole

Throw all of the ingredients in a blender and blend until smooth, season to taste... easy peasey!

Chef's Tip

If you like your food fiery, add 1 or 2 extra chillies to give it a little more heat.

To Serve

Sprinkle with chopped coriander, a little paprika and black pepper. Scatter over some seeds and top with pea shoots.

Ingredients

'Souper' Holy Guacamole

2 ripe avocados (peeled, stone removed)
25g coriander (leaves only)
3 spring onions (topped, tailed, roughly chopped)
1 green chilli (stalk and seeds removed, halved lengthways)
2 tsp hot paprika
500ml vegan stock
6 small yellow tomatoes (peeled, sliced in half, seeds removed)
2 cloves garlic (finely chopped)
2 limes (juice of)
salt and pepper

To Serve

coriander (chopped)
paprika (to dust)
black pepper
pea shoots
sunflower seeds
pumpkin seeds
sesame seeds

POT DOODLE

SERVES 4

🍷 *Viña Real Rioja Blanco, Barrel Fermented
(Spain)*

Ingredients

4 round courgettes

Quinoa And Lentil Mix

2 sweet potatoes
olive oil (good glug of)
salt and pepper (generous seasoning of)
4 sprigs thyme
200g quinoa
100g lentils
400ml vegan stock
4 cloves garlic
5g sage leaves (finely chopped)
5g fresh oregano (finely chopped)
5g mint leaves (finely chopped)
50g red onion (finely chopped)
1½ limes (juice and zest of)
½ lemon (juice of)

For The Fennel Salad

½ red onion
2 bulbs fennel
½ pomegranate
mint (a few sprigs of, leaves only, finely
chopped)
olive oil
½ lemon (juice of)
seasoning

To Serve

lime wedges

Method

For The Quinoa And Lentil Mix

Preheat the oven to 200°C (fan).

Dice the sweet potatoes into 1cm cubes and toss in olive oil.
Roast with a generous pinch of salt, pepper and 2 sprigs of
thyme for 20-25 minutes until tender.

Add the quinoa to boiling, salted water and cook for 10
minutes. Ensure the water is boiling before you add the quinoa!

Boil the lentils for 20 minutes in the vegan stock with 2 sprigs
of thyme and 2 cloves of garlic. Drain and remove the garlic
and thyme.

Combine the sweet potatoes, quinoa and lentils and mix
together well. Heat a good glug of olive oil in a frying pan over
a medium heat, add the remaining garlic, sage, oregano and
mint. Cook gently until the garlic starts to soften. Remove from
the heat and mix in with the other ingredients. Add in the red
onion, lime zest and the lemon and lime juice, season... et voila!

For The Courgette Pots

Preheat the oven to 200°C (fan).

Cut the tops off the courgettes and reserve. Hollow them out
using a spoon.

Roast in the oven for 6-8 minutes, or until slightly softened,
but still structurally intact with a little bite to them. Ovens vary
so keep an eye on them.

For The Fennel Salad

Finely slice the onion and fennel using a mandolin. If you don't
have one, just use a sharp knife and some love!

Hold the flat side of the pomegranate in the palm of your hand
and tap out the kernels using a wooden spoon.

Mix the fennel with the onion, shredded mint and pomegranate
kernels. Toss in a little olive oil, a squeeze of lemon and a pinch
of salt.

To Serve

Fill the courgette pots with your lentil mix and place the lid
back on top. Arrange the fennel salad next to the pots. Finish
with a wedge of lime.

Chef's Tip

If you're struggling to get your hands on round courgettes,
cut normal courgettes horizontally, hollow out each half and
that'll work just as nicely if you stack one half on top of the
other when building your plate. This dish is great served hot
or cold so if you're cooking for guests and want to have
everything prepped before they arrive, this one's a winner.
Some cubed halloumi fried in a little garlic oil goes a long way
tossed in with the quinoa and lentil mix.

JAMAICA IN A JAR

SERVES 4

🍷 *Bottega Gold Prosecco Brut*
(Italy)

Ingredients

Sesame, Chia And Salt Sugar Shards

2 tbsp sesame seeds
2 tbsp chia seeds
Maldon sea salt flakes (few good pinches of)
200g granulated sugar
200ml water

Mango And Lime Base

200g mango chunks
1 lime (juice of)

Coconut Lemon Cream

1 lemon (zest of)
caster sugar
¼ lemon (juice of)
400ml can coconut milk (refrigerated for
6 hours, overnight if possible)
1 tsp vanilla extract
salt (pinch of)

To Serve

chia seeds (sprinkle of)
4 blueberries
4 raspberries

4 x 125ml pots
2 baking trays (lined with parchment)

Method

For The Sesame, Chia And Salt Sugar Shards

Sprinkle the baking sheets with the sesame seeds, chia seeds and a good few pinches of Maldon sea salt flakes.

Bring the sugar and water to the boil until the temperature reaches 153°C.

When the sugar syrup has reached temperature, plunge the pan into some icy water to prevent it cooking further, then quickly and carefully pour a little of the mixture into each lined baking tray, moving and tilting the trays to spread the caramel thinly. Set aside or refrigerate to cool and harden. Once cooled, break roughly into shards, layer them in a sealable container, separating each layer with baking parchment and freeze until required.

> **Chef's Tip**
>
> Make a double batch of the sesame, chia and salt sugar shards. Keep them in an airtight container in the freezer layered with baking parchment. They're great as decorations to jazz up other desserts.

For The Mango And Lime Base

Blend the mango chunks with the lime juice in a blender. Spoon the mixture into each of your pots approximately 1cm deep.

For The Coconut Lemon Cream

Combine the lemon zest and caster sugar in a bowl. Set aside to allow the lemon flavour to infuse into the sugar.

Carefully scoop out the solid coconut cream that has set in the can of coconut milk, reserving the liquid in the bottom. Place in a large mixing bowl with a pinch of salt. Using an electric whisk, starting on a slow speed and gradually increasing to a medium speed, whisk until soft peaks form, approximately 2 minutes. If the coconut cream is too solid and you are unable to get a smooth consistency add a little of the reserved liquid to loosen it. When smooth, add the lemon zest, sugar, lemon juice and vanilla extract. Continue whisking until well combined. Transfer to a piping bag and pipe onto the top of each pot of mango and lime mixture. Pipe a layer approximately 1cm deep so you have equal amounts of mango and coconut cream.

To Serve

Sprinkle each pot with chia seeds. Insert a sesame, chia and salt sugar shard into the centre of each dessert and place 1 blueberry and 1 raspberry on top to finish the pots with some extra colour.

138
HOUSE OF TIDES

28-30 The Close, Quayside, Newcastle Upon Tyne, NE1 3RF

0191 230 3720
www.houseoftides.co.uk Twitter: @houseoftides

Established in February 2014 and set within the beautifully restored Grade I listed 16th Century former merchant's town house, House of Tides is a 50 cover restaurant which is set over two floors. The more rustic ground floor entrance level, with its 16th Century flagstones, provides an excellent venue for a pre-meal drink. The first floor, which houses the main restaurant seating area, has exposed original wood beams and provides the more relaxed and casual setting for your meal.

Double Michelin star chef Kenny Atkinson, together with his wife and business partner Abbie, are passionate about bringing Michelin standard dining to the North East. Kenny's palate for seasonality and sourcing the majority of his ingredients within the British Isles is translated through his classically trained, yet modern day inspired dishes.

Since opening, House of Tides has gained huge support and loyal followers as well as industry acclaim, whilst still being an accessible and relaxed environment. Within its first year, House of Tides was awarded Best Newcomer and North East Restaurant of the Year, as voted by The Journal newspaper's Secret Diner.

In 2015 it was awarded Best Newcomer, voted by the Cateys, as well as being voted 62nd in the top 100 UK restaurants at the National Restaurant Awards and voted 46th best restaurant outside of London by the Square Meal Magazine. House of Tides is also the proud holder of 3 AA Rosettes and Newcastle's only Michelin Star.

House of Tides photographs by Ian Meeson Photography, @IanMeeson01

Holder of Newcastle's only Michelin Star, 3 AA Rosettes and AA England Restaurant of the Year 2015-2016.

MACKEREL, GOOSEBERRIES, LEMON, MUSTARD

SERVES 4

 Clos de Nouys Vouvray (France)

Ingredients

Breaded Mackerel

4 mackerel fillets (pinned, boned, trimmed)
1 tsp English mustard
4 slices white bread
Maldon sea salt (to season)
Borderfields rapeseed oil (to fry)
unsalted butter (to fry)

Gooseberry Purée

250g gooseberries
50g caster sugar
¼ lemon (juice of)
20g unsalted butter
20ml double cream
green food colouring (few drops of)

Lemon Oil

200ml rapeseed oil
2 lemons (zest of)
1 sprig thyme

Gooseberry Jelly

170ml gooseberry wine
40g caster sugar
1g agar agar to 110ml liquid

Pickled Gooseberries

100g fresh gooseberries
50ml gooseberry wine
70ml white wine vinegar
40g caster sugar
1 lemon (zest and juice of)
1 tsp black peppercorns
1 sprig tarragon

Garnish

English red mustard frill cress

Method

For The Breaded Mackerel

Brush a thin layer of mustard onto the skin of the mackerel.

Using a pasta machine, roll the bread out as thin as possible.

Place the fish, mustard-side down, onto the bread and season the fish. Trim the bread to size so you can fold over the fish. Brush the bread with a little mustard and fold over the mackerel to seal.

> **Chef's Tip**
>
> Only buy the freshest mackerel possible from your local fishmonger.

For The Gooseberry Purée

Place the gooseberries, sugar, lemon juice and butter into a vac pac bag and *sous vide* tightly. Cook in a water bath at 70°C for 1 hour. Alternatively, simmer until soft. Remove from the bath and place into a blender. Blitz to a purée and finish with cream and a few drops of food colouring. Pass through a fine sieve and store in a plastic bottle.

For The Lemon Oil

Bring all the ingredients to a simmer in a pan, remove from the heat and leave in a warm area for 6 hours to infuse.

For The Gooseberry Jelly

Bring the wine and sugar to the boil, simmer for 1 minute and leave to cool. When cool, whisk in the agar agar and bring back to a simmer, whisking continuously. Pour into a tray or moulds and allow to chill. Cut to shape and lightly warm the jelly (oven 70°C) before serving. It won't melt, but will have a warm temperature making it nice to eat.

For The Pickled Gooseberries

Bring all the ingredients to the boil, except the gooseberries, then simmer for 5 minutes. Add the gooseberries and bring back to the boil. Remove from the heat and leave to cool.

To Serve

Pan fry the breaded mackerel in a little oil and butter until golden brown on all sides. Pipe a little gooseberry purée onto the plate and swipe a little English mustard. Place the cooked mackerel on top of the mustard, arrange the jelly and pickled gooseberries around the fish, finishing with the mustard cress and a little lemon oil.

LAMB, SPROUTING BROCCOLI, ONIONS, KOHLRABI

SERVES 4

🍷 *Castello Banfi Brunello di Montalcino DOCG 2010, Tuscany (Italy)*

Ingredients

Lamb Rump

1 lamb rump (trimmed), vegetable oil (to seal)
1 sprig rosemary, 3 cloves garlic
butter (knob of), lemon (spritz of)

Braised Shoulder

400g lamb shoulder, 1 tbsp vegetable oil
¼ bunch thyme, ½ bulb garlic (split)
2 fresh bay leaves, 1 tsp black peppercorns
1 carrot, leek, onion (peeled, roughly chopped)
1 stick celery (roughly chopped)
50g tomato purée, 200ml white wine
500ml dark chicken stock

To Finish The Shoulder

20g onion, 20g kohlrabi (both peeled and diced)
20g celery (diced), butter (knob of)
200g braised shoulder (flaked down)
5g mint leaves (chopped)

Lamb Sauce

300g lamb belly (cut into 1cm dice)
1 tbsp vegetable oil
80g each carrots, onions, celery (cut into 1cm dice)
3 cloves garlic, 1 bay leaf, 2g white peppercorns
2 plum tomatoes (chopped)
1 tsp tomato purée, 300ml white wine
500ml lamb braising stock (reserved from shoulder)

Broccoli Purée

1 head broccoli, salt and ground white pepper

Sprouting Broccoli

12 spears sprouting broccoli (trimmed)
lemon oil (drizzle of), salt and pepper (to season)

Marinated Kohlrabi Discs

100ml water
100ml Chardonnay or white wine vinegar
100g caster sugar, 6 sprigs thyme
1 kohlrabi (sliced into discs)

Garnish

grelot onions, sheep's sorrel

Method

For The Lamb Rump

Preheat the oven to 180°C.

Season the lamb and pan roast in very hot oil on all sides. Add the rosemary and garlic and roast in the oven for 10 minutes. Remove from the oven and finish by basting with a little butter and lemon juice. Rest for 8 minutes in a warm area.

For The Braised Shoulder (Prepare in advance)

Preheat the oven to 150°C.

Brown the shoulder in a hot pan with the oil, then place into a deep pot. Add the vegetables , herbs and peppercorns to the same pan and colour until golden. Add the tomato purée and cook out. Transfer to the pot. Pour the wine into the pan, deglaze and reduce by half. Pour over the lamb, add the stock and bring to the boil. Cover and braise in the oven for 4-5 hours. Once cooked, leave to cool in the stock. Remove the lamb and pass the stock through a fine *chinois* and muslin cloth. Reserve for the lamb sauce.

To Finish The Shoulder

Sweat the onions, celery and kohlrabi in the butter until soft. Add the shoulder and mix in, adding a little braising liquor to help bind the shoulder. Finish by stirring in the mint leaves.

For The Lamb Sauce

Caramelise the diced lamb in the oil. Add the vegetables to soften, then add the herbs and spices. Stir in the tomatoes and purée. Deglaze the pan with the wine and reduce to a glaze. Add the reserved stock and simmer for 1 hour. Pass through a double muslin cloth. Skim off any residue or fat on the surface and reduce to a sauce consistency.

For The Broccoli Purée

Cook the broccoli florets in salted, boiling water. Drain and blitz to a smooth purée adding a little cooking liquid if required. Season.

For The Sprouting Broccoli

Blanch in salted, boiling water for 20 seconds, then refresh in iced water. Cut in half and char on top of the stove. Toss in lemon oil and season.

For The Marinated Kohlrabi Discs

Bring all of the ingredients, except the kohlrabi, up to a simmer. Add the kohlrabi and bring back to a simmer. Pour into a deep container and leave to marinate for 1 hour.

For The Grelot Onions

Wash and peel the grelot onions. Cut in half lengthways and pan fry in oil until golden.

To Serve

Serve as pictured.

DARK CHOCOLATE, STRAWBERRIES, ROSEWATER, MERINGUE

SERVES 6

 *Liqueur Muscat
(Australia)*

Ingredients

Wafer Base
240g white chocolate
300g feuilletine wafer flakes

Pave
600g 72% dark chocolate
6 egg yolks, 200g caster sugar
180ml water, 600ml double cream
150ml full-fat milk

Chocolate Jelly
100ml double cream, 100ml water
150g caster sugar, 50g cocoa powder
4 leaves gelatine (softened)
chocolate popping candy (to top)

Strawberry And Rose Jelly
250g strawberries (cored, halved)
90ml water, 20g rose water
40g caster sugar, ½ lemon (juice and zest of)
strawberry liqueur (to taste)
1 leaf gelatine (softened) per 100ml of liquid

Strawberry And Rose Ash Meringues
150g caster sugar
100g egg whites (about 2-3 eggs)
10g cornflour, 5g white wine vinegar
strawberry powder (to dust)

Strawberry Sorbet
400g strawberry purée
100ml water, 150g sugar
20g strawberry liqueur
lemon juice (few drops of)

Marinated Strawberries
strawberries (halved)
1 lemon (juice of), icing sugar (to coat)

Garnish
lemon balm cress

Method

For The Wafer Base
Melt the chocolate and allow to cool before adding the wafer flakes. Fold in and spread between 2 baking sheets. Roll with a rolling pin to form a thin biscuit layer. Set in the fridge in a deep tray.

For The Pave (Prepare in advance)
Whisk the eggs, sugar and water in a bowl over a *bain-marie* until a thick, pale *sabayon* appears. Pour into a food mixer and whisk until thick, pale and cold.

Melt the chocolate to room temperature and pour into the *sabayon*. Semi-whip the milk and cream and whisk half into the chocolate. Fold the remaining cream in carefully and pour over the set base. Chill overnight.

For The Chocolate Jelly
Bring the cream, water and sugar to the boil. Add the cocoa powder and whisk in the gelatine. Allow to cool before pouring over the pave. Chill for 1 hour to set. Top with the popping candy prior to serving.

For The Strawberry And Rose Jelly
Bring the water, rose water, sugar and lemon juice and zest to a simmer. Add the strawberries and leave to infuse. Carefully strain the juice through a fine sieve and muslin cloth. Warm the strained strawberry juice with the liqueur, then stir in the gelatine. Pour the jelly into a deep tray and chill for 2-3 hours to set. Cut into cubes.

For The Strawberry And Rose Ash Meringues
Whisk the egg whites and sugar until stiff and glossy. Add the cornflour and whisk in, then whisk in the vinegar. Spread thinly onto a baking mat, dust with strawberry powder and leave in a hot cupboard until crisp.

For The Strawberry Sorbet
Bring all the ingredients to the boil and simmer lightly for about 5 minutes. Pass through a fine sieve and allow to cool before churning in an ice cream machine.

For The Marinated Strawberries
Toss the strawberries in the lemon juice and sugar and leave for 5 minutes before using.

To Serve
Serve as pictured.

148
HUDSON'S

The Grand Hotel & Spa, Station Rise, York, YO1 6HT

01904 380 038
www.thegrandyork.co.uk Twitter: @theGrandYork @craig_atchinson

As Yorkshire's only 5 star hotel, The Grand Hotel & Spa is synonymous with luxury and the finer things in life. Within view of the York walls and set in the Edwardian splendour of the former headquarters of the North Eastern Railway Company, The Grand is firmly rooted in the city's rich history.

At the heart of The Grand is the award-winning Hudson's restaurant, named after the 'railway king' George Hudson who ensured that York was not left at the station as George Stephenson revolutionised transportation and industrial England.

Hudson's head chef is Craig Atchinson; an adopted local who moved to Yorkshire in 2008 having previously spent 12 years working throughout the UK with some of the country's brightest chefs.

Whilst being respectful of his surrounding's illustrious past, Craig's style is modern British Cuisine which includes a wide range of the latest techniques and classical flavour pairing. The menu is seasonal, taking inspiration from the fruit, vegetables and herbs that are grown in the surrounding areas.

With a passion for game, foraging and gardening, Craig is a perfect fit for the rural county where he can source all his ingredients. Local grouse, rabbit, fish and wild edible ingredients all feature on the restaurant's menu.

Craig ensures that every diner, whether a hotel resident or visiting guest, is served only the very best.

Hudson's restaurant in the heart of York's 5 star hotel, The Grand Hotel & Spa, offers modern fine dining served in an elegant setting, combining heritage and history with contemporary luxury to create a unique ambience and dining experience.

HAND DIVED SCALLOPS, WAKAME, PICKLED CUCUMBER, DILL MAYONNAISE

SERVES 4

🍷 *Albariño, Rias Baixas, Valmiñor, Galicia 2013 (Spain)*

Ingredients

Scallops
8 hand dived scallops (removed from the shell)
lemon juice (spritz of)

Dill Mayonnaise
1 bunch fresh dill
200ml vegetable oil
2 egg yolks
1 tbsp Dijon mustard

Wakame
100g dried wakame
lemon juice (spritz of)
salt (pinch of)

Pickled Cucumber
100g cucumber (skin on, seeds removed)
50ml white wine vinegar
50g caster sugar
100ml water

Garnish
raw sea herbs (arrowgrass, rock samphire, sea aster)
salmon keta
sunflower seeds

Method

For The Scallops
Use an oyster shucking knife, place it at the hinge of the scallop, prizing it open slightly. Turn over and run a flexible fish filleting knife over the flat side of the shell to release the scallop. Open the shell fully. Use a spoon to release the scallop from the bottom shell. Pull off the frill, the black stomach sack and any other pieces that are around the meat of the scallop and discard, leaving just the white flesh. Rinse thoroughly in cold water. Season with salt and sear in a hot pan for a couple of minutes on each side. Finish with a few drops of lemon juice.

> **Chef's Tip**
>
> Ask your fishmonger to remove the scallops from the shell. Do this as close as possible to serving time to be sure they are as fresh as they can be.

For The Dill Mayonnaise
Blanch the dill for 10 seconds in salted boiling water, then squeeze out the excess water in a cloth. Blend the dill and oil in a powerful liquidiser for 2 minutes. Strain the oil through a muslin cloth. Place the egg yolks and Dijon mustard in a mixing bowl and whisk well to break the yolks. Slowly add the dill oil whilst continuously whisking until all of the oil is incorporated. Season with salt. Reserve in the fridge.

For The Wakame
Pour boiling water onto the dried seaweed and steep for 10 minutes to rehydrate (you can do this the day before). Just before serving, warm in a small pan and season with lemon juice and salt.

For The Pickled Cucumber
Finely shred the cucumber using a Japanese mandolin. Bring the vinegar, sugar and water to the boil, then pour the hot liquid onto the shredded cucumber. Allow to cool to room temperature.

To Assemble
Spoon some of the seaweed onto one side of your desired serving plates, add a small amount of the pickled cucumber on top of this. Once the scallops are cooked, cut 1 in half to give an extra dimension to the plate and arrange on top of the seaweed and cucumber. Randomly dot the dill mayonnaise and garnish as you wish.

WATERFORD FARM BEEF, SMOKED SIRLOIN, BRAISED CHEEK, ONION PUREE, WOODLAND MUSHROOMS

SERVES 4

 Toscana Rosso, Villa Cafaggio, San Martino Vineyard, Tuscany 2003 (Italy)

Ingredients

Smoked Sirloin

1kg beef striploin (cut into a barrel shape, connective tissue removed)
beech wood smoked chips (hickory and oak are also good)

Beef Cheeks

2 large beef cheeks
300ml red wine
1 carrot (peeled, chopped)
1 onion (peeled, chopped)
1 sprig thyme
3 cloves garlic
1 litre beef stock

Onion Purée

500g onions (sliced)
125g unsalted butter
75ml double cream

To Serve

wild mushrooms (lightly sautéed)
grelot onions (chargrilled)
turnips (charred, buttered)
nasturtium leaves, edible flowers (optional)

Method

For The Smoked Sirloin

Use a suitable roasting tray to smoke the beef - the tray will need to be big enough to sit a cooling rack in. Add the smoking chips into the tray, then place the beef barrel on the cooling rack. Heat the tray on an open gas flame until the chips begin to smoulder. Once there is a good amount of smoke, turn down the heat and cover the tray with tin foil. Smoke for 3 minutes, then turn off the heat. Allow the tray to fully cool before uncovering. Once cool enough to handle, wrap the beef tightly in cling film and chill for 2 hours to retain its shape. Cut into 4 equal portions and roast in a hot pan to your liking; medium rare is recommended as this cut will be tender.

> **Chef's Tip**
>
> Don't compromise with quality. Ask your butcher for providence on your meat.

For The Beef Cheeks (Prepare in advance)

Ask your butcher to remove any skin/sinew from the cheeks as this is very tricky to do. Cut each cheek in half and cover with the wine in a suitable container. Add the vegetables, thyme and garlic and marinate overnight. Remove the cheeks from the marinade and pat dry. Brown the cheeks in a hot pan until golden and caramelised. Add the browned cheeks to a large saucepan with the marinade, vegetables and stock and bring to the boil. Simmer for 4-6 hours or until the cheeks are very tender. Remove the meat from the pan. Strain the cooking liquid into a clean pan, then reduce until very thick and sticky. Place the cheeks back in the pan to glaze in the reduced stock.

For The Onion Purée

Warm the butter until foaming in a medium sized saucepan, add the sliced onions and cook very slowly until golden, about 1-2 hours. Once coffee coloured, add the cream and bring to the boil. Blend in a high powered liquidiser until very smooth, pass through a sieve and season with salt to taste.

To Serve

Spoon a generous amount of the purée at one end of the serving plates and swipe with a dessert spoon. Place the glazed beef cheek in the centre. Slice the smoked sirloin into bite size pieces and fan around the cheek. Finish with the vegetables and garnish as desired.

INSPIRATION OF 'FERRERO ROCHER'

SERVES 4

🍷 *Skillogalee, Liqueur Muscat, Clare Valley (Australia)*

Ingredients

Rocher
250g dark chocolate 70%
2 eggs yolks
360ml double cream
nibbed almonds

Praline Paste
150g praline paste
200ml skimmed milk

Candied Pistachios
150g pistachios
80g icing sugar

Rocher Coating
60g dark chocolate 70%
40g cocoa butter
edible gold paint

8 half sphere moulds (58mm diameter, 31mm deep)

Method

For The Rocher (Prepare ahead)

Melt the chocolate over a *bain-marie*. Once fully melted, bring 80ml of the cream to the boil. Meanwhile, whisk the remaining cream to soft peaks. Add the egg yolks to the melted chocolate and beat well (don't worry if it looks split). Pour over the boiled cream, beat again, then fold in the lightly whipped cream. Pipe into half sphere moulds and freeze, minimum 4 hours.

For The Praline Paste

Simply mix the praline paste and skimmed milk together. Place in a piping bag until needed.

For The Candied Pistachios

Preheat the oven to 180°C.

Roast the pistachios in the oven for 6-8 minutes until golden. Remove, then add a small amount of water, just enough to coat the nuts. Toss the nuts, sieving the icing sugar over, then return to the oven for 5 more minutes. Allow to cool.

To Assemble

Once the mousse (Rocher) has frozen, scoop out the centre with a melon baller, then fill with praline paste. Return to the freezer until the praline has frozen solid. Remove the half spheres from the moulds. Push 2 half spheres together, then roll in nibbed almonds.

For The Rocher Coating

Melt the dark chocolate with the cocoa butter to thin it out. Dip the spheres in the melted chocolate, then chill. Spray with edible gold paint for a luxurious finish.

To Serve

Allow to come to room temperature so that the praline centre is liquid. Serve as pictured.

> **Chef's Tip**
>
> Use a really good quality chocolate for this recipe - either Valrhona or Michel Cluizel.

158
THE JOLLY FISHERMAN

9 Haven Hill, Craster, Alnwick, Northumberland, NE66 3TR

01665 576 461
www.thejollyfishermancraster.co.uk

The Jolly Fisherman, Craster, combines stunning sea views with delicious home cooking and beautifully kept ales. A tastefully refurbished pub with tradition and character at its heart.

Great care has been taken to retain the charm of this historic pub with stone flagged floors, low beamed ceilings and comfortable seating.

Large sliding windows, overlooking the harbour, give the feeling of being outside. Enjoy the terrace and beer garden during the summer months, with unrivalled views of the coastline and during the winter, relax by the roaring, open fires.

Fresh crab and lobster is delivered daily from the last remaining fishing boat out of Craster. Local game and meats are sourced from surrounding Northumberland estates.

The Jolly Fisherman was established by Charles Archbold in 1847. Over the past 165 years, the building has grown in both size and reputation and is popular with locals, coastal ramblers and day-trippers alike.

Following a full refurbishment in 2012, new publican David Whitehead and his team are

proud to continue and enhance the rich, culinary heritage of one of Northumberland's most iconic destinations. 'The Jolly Fisherman on the Quay' opens its doors in 2016, a state-of-the-art gastro pub overlooking the Tyne bridges with views to 'dine' for!

The Jolly Fisherman achieved 'Best Pub in Northumberland Award 2015' at the What's on Where Awards.

DELICATE SALAD OF SMOKED EEL, CARROLL'S HERITAGE NEW POTATOES, POACHED CHATTON FARM EGG

SERVES 4

🍷 *Picpoul de Pinet, 2012, Domaine Felines Jourdan (France)*

Ingredients

250g smoked eel

Vinaigrette
1 tsp wholegrain mustard
1 tsp soft brown sugar
1 tbsp white wine vinegar
pomace oil (to loosen)
salt and pepper (to taste)

Salad
1 curly endive
4 Carroll's Heritage new potatoes (cooked, sliced)
4 baby vine tomatoes (quartered)
4 Chatton Farm free range eggs

To Finish
50g micro fennel

Method

For The Vinaigrette

Mix the mustard, sugar and vinegar in a bowl. Add enough pomace oil to make a pouring consistency. Season with salt and pepper.

For The Salad

Break up the centre of the curly endive and place it in a large bowl with the potatoes and tomatoes. Mix together with the vinaigrette.

For The Smoked Eel

Preheat the oven to 180°C.

Warm the eel in the oven for 2 minutes.

> **Chef's Tip**
> Lightly warm the eel to make it easier to break up for the salad.

To Finish And Serve

Divide the salad between 4 bowls. Break the eel on top of the salads. Bring a pan of water to the boil and add a little vinegar. Carefully poach the eggs for 3 minutes, taking care not to break the yolks.

Place an egg on top of each salad and finish by sprinkling with micro fennel.

TART OF NORTHUMBRIAN GAME WITH ROASTED WINTER VEGETABLES, QUINCE JELLY, RED WINE JUS

SERVES 4

Madiran, Château d'Aydie, 2012
(South West France)

Ingredients

Game Filling

4 x 90g loin of venison
4 grouse breasts
4 pheasant breasts
oil (glug of)
butter (knob of)
salt (pinch of)

Pastry Tart Case

125g self-raising flour
65g unsalted butter
1 tsp water
salt (to season)

Winter Vegetables

2 parsnips
2 carrots
2 red onions
2 beetroot
oil (drizzle of)

Quince Jelly

3 quince
250ml port
250ml water
salt (pinch of)
pepper (pinch of)
3g sugar
3 leaves gelatine (softened)

Red Wine Jus

residue juice from resting meats
25ml red wine
1 tsp quince jelly
salt and pepper (to taste)

Garnish

50g curly kale, micro rocket

4 tart cases

Method

For The Game Filling

Sauté the meat in a pan with oil, butter and salt for 10 minutes or until the meat is pink. Leave to rest.

> **Chef's Tip**
>
> Cook the venison first and leave to rest.

For The Pastry Tart Case

Preheat the oven to 180°C.

Mix the flour and butter together with touch of water and salt to a paste consistency. Leave to rest for 20 minutes.

Roll the pastry out and divide into 4 pastry tart cases. Blind bake for 5 minutes, remove baking beans and bake for a further 3 minutes. Leave to cool.

For The Winter Vegetables

Preheat the oven to 180°C.

Peel the vegetables and roughly chop. Drizzle with oil, season and bake for 15-20 minutes until cooked.

For The Quince Jelly

Poach the quince in the port and boiling water with the sugar, salt and pepper. Cook until soft to touch. Add the softened gelatine to the pan and leave to cool, then set in the fridge for 2 hours.

For The Red Wine Jus

Reduce the juices from the resting meats with the red wine and quince jelly. Season to taste.

To Serve

Arrange the roasted vegetables inside the tart case. Rest the meats on top of the vegetables and pour the red wine jus over. Place a tablespoon of quince jelly on top of the meats and finish with a garnish of micro rocket and a serving of kale.

RICH CHOCOLATE SOUFFLE

SERVES 4

🍷 *Maury, Domaine Lafage, 2013, Roussillon (France)*

Ingredients

Chocolate Soufflé

100g dark chocolate
60g cocoa powder
150ml cold water
8 egg whites
60g caster sugar

To Coat The Ramekins

1 tsp unsalted butter
1 tbsp caster sugar
1 tbsp cocoa powder

To Serve

icing sugar
vanilla ice cream
raspberries

4 ramekins

Method

To Prepare The Ramekins

Melt the butter and brush inside the ramekins in an upward motion. Mix the sugar and cocoa powder together and sprinkle into each ramekin until coated, shaking off any excess.

> **Chef's Tip**
> When coating the ramekins with butter, move the pastry brush in an upwards motion.

For The Chocolate Soufflé

Preheat the oven to 190°C.

Melt the chocolate in a bowl suspended over a saucepan of simmering water.

Mix the cocoa powder with the cold water, bring to the boil, then transfer into the melted chocolate. Keep this warm.

Whisk the egg whites to soft peaks, then add quarter of the egg whites to the chocolate mixture and blend in. Gently fold in the remaining egg whites with a metal spoon, taking care not to knock the air out.

Fill each prepared ramekin to the rim, using a palate knife to level off. Bake the soufflés for 10-15 minutes. Do not open the oven door.

To Serve

Dust the serving plates with icing sugar. Decorate with some fresh raspberries and serve with a scoop of vanilla ice cream. Place the soufflés on the plates and serve immediately.

168
KO SAI

Fenwick Food Hall, Northumberland Street, Newcastle, NE1 7AS

0191 239 6612
www.ko-sai.co.uk Twitter: @_KO_Sai Facebook: Ko_Sai

K o Sai is a chic, lively noodle bar that brings South East Asian street food to shoppers and diners in Newcastle.

Located within the spectacular new food hall of the city's biggest department store, Fenwick, Ko Sai is already winning positive reviews since opening in October 2015.

This restaurant is a joint venture between renowned chef and restaurateur Terry Laybourne and Thai-born award-winning chef Parichat Somsri-Kirby, who has worked at Café 21 at Fenwick since it opened in 2006.

Pla, as she is better known by many, has worked alongside Terry since 2000 and has always had a dream of one day running her own restaurant; particularly one focussed on Pan-Asian food flavours that she grew up with and the dishes cooked by her mother on the family rice farm in Thailand.

This fashionable noodle-bar offers fast, casual dining at counter seats. The food is big on flavour, fresh and healthy. The menu is flexible, offering finger food snacks as well as hot dishes and cold, refreshing salads. These can be washed down with a glass of wine, a fresh juice or the house beer, which has been developed in conjunction with regional craft brewer, Wylam Brewery.

The menu features some of the favourite flavours found in Cambodia, China, Vietnam, Thailand and Korea - packed with fragrant ingredients such as lemongrass, ginger, coriander, kaffir lime and coconut. Dishes include soup noodles, stir fries and curries, steamed buns and fresh flavoured Thai and Vietnamese style salads.

Ko-Sai is open 11am-8pm Monday to Saturday; 11am-4pm Sunday.

Chic and lively, Ko Sai is a new Pan-Asian street food influenced noodle bar within Newcastle's Fenwick Food Hall. This fashionable venue is a joint venture run by renowned chef and restaurateur Terry Laybourne and Thai-born award-winning chef Parichat Somsri-Kirby.

PRAWN, GREEN MANGO & CASHEW NUT SALAD

SERVES 4

Ko Sai Pilsner 3.8%
Wylam Brewery (UK)

Ingredients

340g small king prawns (shelled, deveined)

Prawn Poaching Liquor

400ml water
½ tsp salt
1 tsp sugar
½ lime leaf
½ tbsp lime juice
½ small lemongrass stalk (bruised)
10g coriander stalks (bruised)
½ clove garlic (crushed)
1 shallot (slice)

Green Mango Salad

1 green mango (peeled, stoned, cut into *julienne*)
16 cherry tomatoes (quartered)
120g cucumber (peeled, deseeded, cut into *julienne*)
120g French beans (*blanched* for 2 minutes in boiling, salted water)
40g spring onions (*julienne*)
40g coriander (picked, washed)
40g mint (picked, washed)
200g Chinese cabbage (finely sliced)
40g salted cashew nuts (lightly toasted)

Dressing

2 cloves garlic (peeled, finely grated)
2 long red chillies (deseeded, finely sliced)
2 long green chillies (deseeded, finely sliced)
40g palm sugar (grated)
30ml lime juice
60ml Thai fish sauce

Method

For The Prawn Poaching Liquor

Bring everything to the boil and simmer for 5-10 minutes. Remove from the heat and allow to stand for 10 minutes before passing through a fine strainer.

For The Prawns

Bring the poaching liquid to the boil and add the prawns. Stir with a metal spoon, remove the pan from the heat and leave to cool before draining.

For The Dressing

Stir everything together in a small bowl until the sugar has dissolved.

For The Green Mango Salad

Mix all of the salad ingredients together in a large bowl. Add the dressing and toss well.

To Serve

Divide the salad evenly between 4 salad bowls. Top with the poached prawns.

SPICY CHICKEN COCONUT BROTH, RICE NOODLE, SOFT EGG, CABBAGE & CRISPY SHALLOTS

SERVES 4

 Les Saisonnier 5.4%, Belgian-style, lemon balm and rosemary saison ale, Wylam Brewery (UK)

Ingredients

Red Curry Coconut Broth

2 tbsp vegetable oil
2 tbsp red curry paste
33g palm sugar
1 litre coconut milk
2 small lime leaves
1 stalk lemongrass
1 tbsp Thai fish sauce
330ml chicken stock

Crispy Shallots

3 shallots
flour (to dust)
oil (to deep fry)

To Finish

4 eggs (boiled for 6 minutes, then shocked in iced water)
120g rice noodles (soaked in lots of water for 40-50 minutes)
120g bean sprouts
120g white cabbage (finely shredded)
2 chicken breasts (skinned, poached, sliced)
24g coriander (picked, rinsed)
80g spring onions (*julienne*)

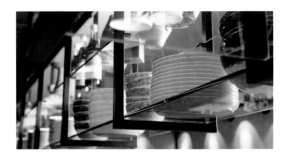

Method

For The Red Curry Coconut Broth

Heat the oil in a saucepan, add the curry paste and fry gently for 2 minutes. Add the palm sugar and cook for 1 minute. Pour in 250ml of coconut milk, add the lime leaves, lemongrass and fish sauce and cook for 2 minutes.

Add half of the chicken stock and another 500ml of coconut milk and bring to the boil for 5 minutes. Add the remaining stock and coconut milk, then simmer gently for 10 minutes.

Remove from the heat and set aside.

For The Crispy Shallots

Peel the shallots and slice very finely into rings. Press dry on kitchen paper, then toss in flour. Shake off any excess flour and fry in oil (160°C) until golden and crispy. Drain on a paper towel.

To Finish And Serve

Carefully remove the shells from the soft boiled eggs. Reheat the broth and add the chicken.

Cook the soaked rice noodles in a pot of boiling water for 2 minutes, then drain and divide between 4 serving bowls. Ladle the broth over, placing the chicken on top.

Arrange the bean sprouts, cabbage, soft egg, coriander, spring onions and crispy shallots as pictured. Serve immediately with chopsticks and a large soup spoon.

ICED BANANA & PASSION FRUIT MACAROON

MAKES 8 PIECES

Ingredients

Iced Banana And Passion Fruit Parfait

170g caster sugar
90g egg whites (from 2-3 eggs)
6 passion fruit
1 banana (peeled, cut into chunks)
600ml whipping cream (semi whipped)
1 leaf gelatine (soaked)

Macaroons

170g ground almonds
170g icing sugar
190g granulated sugar
5 egg whites
yellow food colouring (a knife point of)

22cm square baking tray (chilled, lined with cling film)

Method

For The Iced Banana And Passion Fruit Parfait
(Prepare the day before)

Add a little cold water to the sugar in a heavy bottomed pan. Bring to the boil, stirring to dissolve. Place a sugar thermometer in the pan and continue to heat.

Whisk the egg whites slowly in a mixer until they begin to whiten.

Check the temperature of the sugar and when it reaches 90°C increase the speed of the mixer.

When the sugar reaches 121°C carefully pour onto the whisked whites and add the gelatine. Continue whisking until cold.

Halve the passion fruits and scoop the centres out into a food processor. Process for 1 minute to release all of the pulp from the seeds. Force through a fine sieve and measure out 60ml.

Process the banana chunks with the passion fruit purée. Fold this mixture into the meringue mix using a rubber spatula. Gently fold in the whipped cream. Spread the mixture evenly to a thickness of around 15mm. Freeze overnight.

Cut into discs using a 65mm pastry cutter. Return to the freezer, stored in an airtight container between pieces of silicone paper.

For The Macaroons

Preheat the oven to 140°C.

Place the ground almonds and icing sugar in a liquidiser and process to a fine powder. Pass through a fine sieve onto a sheet of greaseproof paper.

Bring the granulated sugar to the boil with a little cold water and continue cooking to 118°C. Remove from the heat.

Whisk 3 of the egg whites until light ribbons begin to form. Pour in the cooked sugar very slowly. Continue whisking for 10 minutes before adding the food colouring. Whisk for a further 2 minutes.

Combine the almond mixture with the remaining 2 egg whites to form a paste. Fold into the meringue mix, then transfer to a piping bag.

Using a 75mm pastry cutter as a guide, draw a series of circles onto a sheet of non-stick baking paper. Invert the paper onto a flat baking sheet and pipe the mixture into discs. Set aside for 20 minutes to allow a fine skin to form.

Bake for 8 minutes. Remove from the oven and slide the paper immediately off the tray onto your worktop. Allow to cool thoroughly. Store in an airtight container.

To Serve

Simply sandwich 1 disc of parfait between 2 macaroons.

178
LONGSANDS FISH KITCHEN

27 Front Street, Tynemouth, Tyne & Wear, NE30 4DZ

0191 272 8552 www.longsandsfishkitchen.com
Twitter: @LongsandsFish Facebook: Longsands Fish Kitchen Instagram: LongsandsFish

Since opening in the summer of 2015, Longsands Fish Kitchen has quickly established itself as a destination for seafood lovers. The restaurant is in the beautiful coastal village of Tynemouth, only a stone's throw away from the local fish quay and the stunning Northumberland coastline.

Whether it is grilled turbot served in the restaurant, or classic fish and chips served from the takeaway, fish is at the heart of every dish.

The menu is dictated by what has been caught that day by the local fishermen on the North East Coast. They are fortunate that the fish and shellfish can go from sea to plate in a matter of hours.

Because fish is highly seasonal, it provides a unique challenge to the chefs. Once they know what fish has been landed, the chefs work on drawing in other seasonal ingredients to shape the dishes.

Longsands Fish Kitchen has a vibrant atmosphere, attracting a wide audience from locals and tourists to seafood enthusiasts from all over the country. The takeaway offers both traditional British favourites and a few unexpected additions such as spiced shrimp burger and salt and pepper squid, including their own brand of Fish Kitchen sauces. They strive to keep regular diners coming back for more by being continually inventive with their menu. Here they are delighted to share three of their most popular dishes with you.

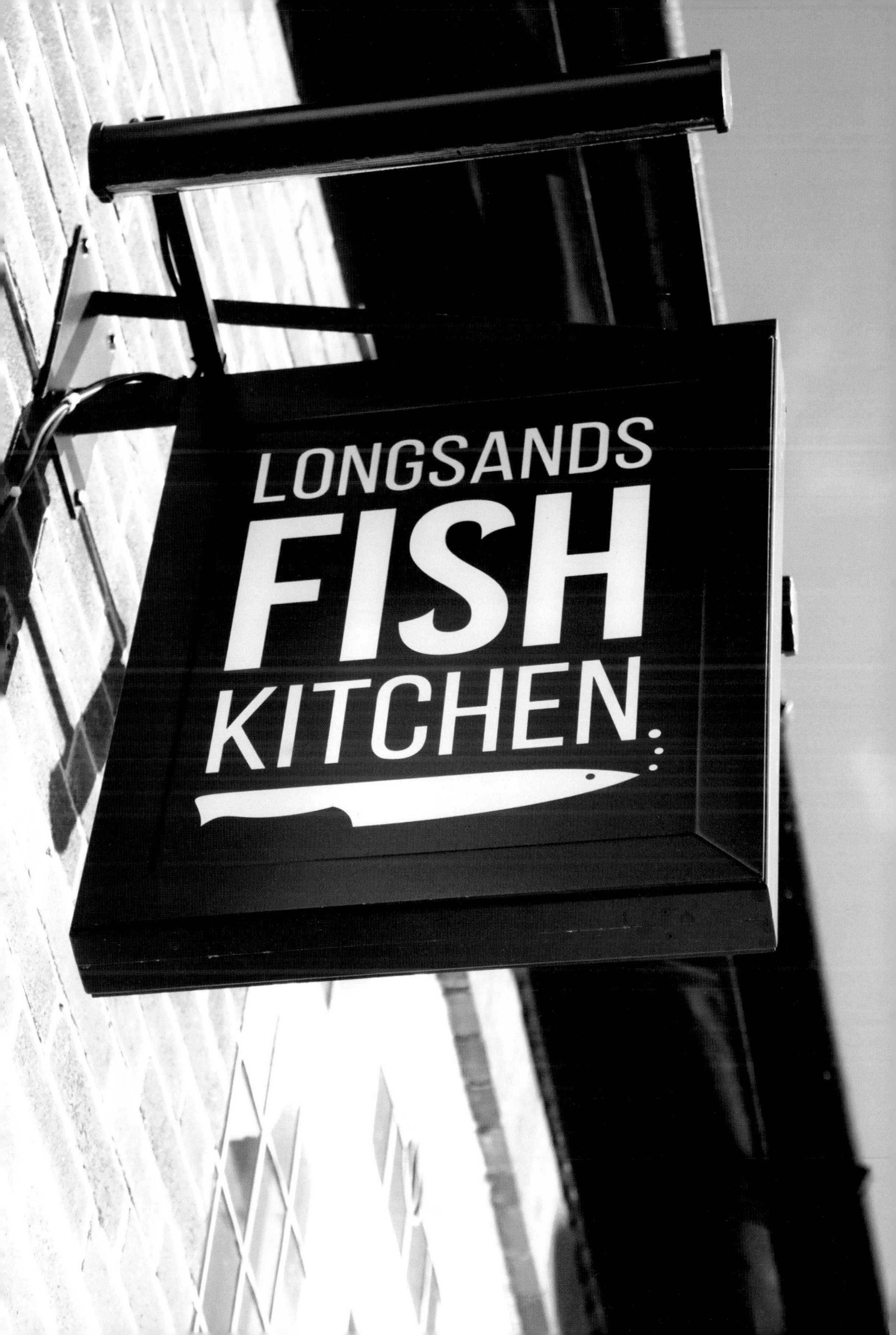
LONGSANDS
FISH
KITCHEN.

Having the restaurant so close to the North Shields Fish Quay, Longsands Fish Kitchen is spoilt for choice, with some of the finest fish on the North East coast landed here every day.

WET YOUR WHISTLE!

OCTOPUS SALAD

SERVES 4

🍷 *Veigadares Albariño 2012, Adegas Galegas (Spain)*

Ingredients

Octopus Terrine

2kg octopus
2 carrots (chopped)
1 onion (diced)
1 bay leaf
300ml fresh orange juice
2 litres water
2 leaves gelatine (soaked)
568ml reserved cooking liquor
2 tbsp dill (chopped)
1 tbsp red chilli (diced)
1 orange (zest of)
sea salt (to taste)

Pickled Cucumber

½ cucumber (thinly sliced)
100ml water
100ml white wine vinegar
100g caster sugar

Garnish

1 red chilli (diced)
3 breakfast radish (finely sliced)
1 spring onion (sliced)
2 sprigs coriander
lemon oil (drizzle of)

Method

For The Octopus Terrine (Prepare ahead)

Place the octopus, carrot, onion, bay leaf, orange juice and water in a heavy bottomed pan over a high heat. Once the pan comes to a boil, lower the heat and simmer for 2-3 hours. Every now and again, skim the impurities from the surface of the liquid and discard.

Once your octopus is cooked, take the pan off the heat and leave to cool. Strain through a sieve, saving 568ml of the cooking liquor.

Use the back of a small knife to peel away the dark skin from the body and legs, making sure you get right in between the tentacles leaving only the white meat. Remove the legs keeping them whole and chop up the head and body meat.

Whisk the soaked gelatine into the reserved cooking liquor. Mix the octopus meat with the dill, chilli, zest, sea salt and cooking liquor and roll up into a sausage shape with cling film. Chill in the fridge overnight.

Chef's Tip

Freeze the octopus, removing the beak and ink sack, for 48 hours before use. This helps tenderise the octopus.

For The Pickled Cucumber

Bring the water, vinegar and sugar to a simmer. Once the sugar has dissolved, take off the heat and cool. Pour over the cucumber.

To Plate

Thinly slice the terrine, remove the cling film and arrange 7 slices on each plate. Mix all the garnish ingredients together and scatter over the top.

FISH KITCHEN PIE

SERVES 4

🍷 *Macon-Verze 2013, Domaines Leflaive, Burgundy (France)*

Ingredients

Fish

250g cod fillet (cut into 25g pieces)
200g salmon fillet (cut into 25g pieces)
200g natural smoked haddock (diced)
4 large scallops (cut in half)
20 mussels (cooked)
4 langoustine tails
20g shrimps
2 tbsp chives (chopped)

White Sauce

45g unsalted butter
55g plain flour
700ml milk
1 bay leaf
2 cloves
1 tsp salt
black pepper (pinch of)

To Finish The Sauce

30g unsalted butter
200g onion (finely diced)
100g carrot (finely diced)
100g celery (finely diced)
100ml white wine
100ml double cream
1 lemon (juice of)
salt and pepper

Mashed Potato

800g potato (peeled, diced)
2 tsp salt
150g unsalted butter
100ml milk (warm)
nutmeg (freshly grated, to taste)
3 egg yolks

To Finish

40g Gruyère cheese (grated)
20g Parmesan (grated)
2 tbsp chives (chopped)
4 langoustine heads

4 pie dishes

Method

For The White Sauce

Melt the butter in a pan on a low heat. Add the flour and cook for 5 minutes while stirring. Meanwhile, place the milk in a pan with the bay leaf, cloves and bring to just below the boil. Pour the milk into the flour, a little at a time, stirring all the time. Season and cook out for 5 minutes.

To Finish The Sauce

Melt the butter in a pan and add all the vegetables. Cook for 5 minutes without colouring Stir in the wine and reduce by two thirds. Add the white sauce, cream, lemon juice and seasoning. Simmer for 2 minutes, stirring all the time. Remove from the heat.

To Make The Mashed Potato

Cover the diced potato with cold water and 1½ teaspoons of salt. Place on the heat and bring to the boil. Simmer until the potatoes are cooked. Drain the potatoes really well. Put the potatoes back into the pan to dry out. Mash, adding the butter, remaining salt and warm milk. Once smooth, remove from the heat, add the nutmeg and egg yolks. Put the mash into a piping bag fitted with a star nozzle.

To Finish

Preheat the oven to 180°C (fan).

Add the fish to the hot sauce, cook lightly for 30 seconds, then add the scallops, langoustine tails, mussels, shrimps and chives. Divide between 4 pie dishes and pipe with the potato. Sprinkle with the grated cheeses, place a langoustine head in the middle of each pie and bake for 15 minutes until golden. Sprinkle with chives and serve.

Chef's Tip

If you can't get scallops or langoustines, use monkfish and king prawns instead.

CHILLED CHOCOLATE FONDANT, ROASTED BANANA ICE CREAM & TOFFEE SAUCE

SERVES 4

🍷 *San Emilio Pedro Ximénez Solera Reserva,
Emilio Lustau, Jerez (Spain)*

Ingredients

Chocolate Fondant

600g dark chocolate
100g unsalted butter
100g cocoa powder
6 medium eggs
6 egg yolks
300g caster sugar
200ml water
700ml double cream (whisked to soft peaks)

Sesame Wafers

25g golden syrup
75g unsalted butter
75g Demerara sugar
25ml full-fat milk
25g ground almonds
30g sesame seeds

Roasted Banana Ice Cream

4 medium bananas (peeled)
125g caster sugar
500ml full-fat milk
500ml double cream
10 egg yolks
25ml liquid glucose
salt (pinch of)
30ml Crème de Banane liqueur

Toffee Sauce

100g caster sugar
50ml water
50ml double cream
25g salted butter

8 moulds

Method

For The Chocolate Fondant

Combine the chocolate, butter and cocoa powder in a bowl and melt over a pan of simmering water. Whisk together the eggs and yolks until white and fluffy using a mixer. While the eggs are mixing, combine the sugar and water in a small pan and bring to 116°C. Once the sugar reaches the required temperature, pour slowly into the eggs whilst the mixer is still running. Leave the mixer on a medium speed while the egg mixture cools. Gently fold the egg mixture into the chocolate, then add the cream. Place in the moulds and set in the fridge.

For The Sesame Wafers

Put the golden syrup, butter and Demerara sugar in a small pan and heat gently until the sugar has dissolved. Add the milk and leave to cool a little. Mix in the ground almonds and sesame seeds. Chill for 30 minutes.

Preheat the oven to 180°C (fan).

Spread the mixture onto a baking mat on a baking sheet. Bake for 4-5 minutes until golden brown. Remove from the oven and cool. Break into jagged pieces.

For The Roasted Banana Ice Cream

Preheat the oven to 180°C (fan).

Coat the bananas in 50g of the sugar, transfer to a buttered baking tray and roast for 20 minutes until golden brown. Gently bring the milk and cream to the boil. Meanwhile, whisk the egg yolks with the glucose, salt and remaining sugar until pale and creamy. Pour half the milk mixture onto the egg yolks, whisking to combine, then pour this back into the saucepan. Cook over a gentle heat, stirring constantly, until the mixture thickens enough to coat the back of a spoon. Remove from the heat and blend with the roasted bananas until smooth. Strain through a fine sieve, then stir in the Crème de Banane. Churn in an ice cream machine and freeze.

For The Toffee Sauce

Combine the sugar and water in a small pan over a medium heat. Boil until the liquid turns a golden brown colour. Whisk in the cream, followed by the butter to finish.

To Serve

Remove the fondants from the moulds and place on the plate. Drizzle toffee sauce around it. Serve with a scoop of banana ice cream and a shard of sesame wafer.

> **Chef's Tip**
> Lightly blow torch the chocolate fondant to give it a lovely, shiny finish.

188
LORD CREWE ARMS
AT BLANCHLAND

The Square, Blanchland, Consett, County Durham, DH8 9SP

01434 675 469
www.lordcrewearmsblanchland.co.uk Twitter: @Lord_Crewe_Arms

Cosseted by the wilds of the Pennine Moors, The Lord Crewe Arms sits snug on the Northumberland Durham border. Enjoying some of the very best views that the North has to offer, you don't have to look far for an excuse to head out (and up!) to sample its delights. So, go on, hit the road, drink in the moorland heather and just as you get to the tops, that's when you will spot it, a 12th Century abbots' guest house nuzzled in the nooks of the valley village of Blanchland; all ready, set, to shake up any preconception you may already have of country living.

Opening its doors in the spring of 2014, this pub/eatery/cosy country bolt hole has chef Simon Hicks at the kitchen's helm (or the engine room as he likes to call it). Bossing his brigade of buzzy, young talent, Simon's food is all about losing the shenanigans and instead, plating up simple dishes that are packed full of imaginative flavours. With a quiet nod to the good old days, the ever changing menu (yes, they like to keep staff on their toes) shouts seasonality with a few 'naughty' Crewe twists...

Otherwise known as 'The Band of Brothers'
The Crewe's team has Simon 'how long for
my tea' Hicks, Jared 'cake maker/heart breaker'
Bell, Steve 'big green egg' Burkitt, Matthew
'Marley' Jones, Andy 'checking the scores'
Gaynor, Helen 'see ya later' Lee, Mr Stuie
'zumba' Douglas and Jamie 'magpie' Pearce.

BAR

FRESH CRAB & PICKLED CUCUMBER SALAD

SERVES 4

🍷 *Saint-Aubin 'Champ Tirant' Gerard Thomas 2012*
Burgundy (France)

Ingredients

Crab Salad

160g white crab meat (picked)
10g chives (chopped)
60g red chicory
20g sea aster
salt and pepper (to season)

Pickled Cucumber

50ml Chardonnay vinegar
icing sugar (to taste)
40g cucumber

Dressing

20ml Chardonnay vinegar
100ml rapeseed oil (extra virgin)
1 lemon (juice of)
1 sprig tarragon

Method

For The Pickled Cucumber

Bring the Chardonnay vinegar to the boil, then remove from the heat. Whisk in the icing sugar until you have a sweet and sour taste - the amount of icing sugar needed will depend on the type and quality of vinegar you use. Leave to chill, then soak the cucumber in the liquid for 30 minutes.

To Make The Dressing

Simply add the vinegar to the oil and lemon juice. Give it a good whisk, then add the tarragon after the dressing is made.

For The Crab Salad

Combine all the ingredients plus the pickled cucumber in a large bowl. Mix together and dress well. Season with salt and pepper and arrange on the plate.

> **Chef's Tip**
>
> Buy the best picked crab you can: look for a bright white flesh which is not too wet, or buy a 500g cock (male) crab to cook yourself.

PAN FRIED MONKFISH TAIL WITH CURRIED TOMATOES

SERVES 4

Dr Loosen Wehlener Sonnenuhr Riesling Auslese 2009 (Germany)

Ingredients

Monkfish

480g monkfish (on or off the bone, seasoned)
20ml vegetable oil

Curried Tomatoes

300g onions (chopped)
40ml vegetable oil
2 cloves garlic (chopped)
1 red chilli (chopped)
25g ginger (chopped)
2 tsp ground coriander
2 tsp ground cumin
3 tsp garam masala
1 tsp curry powder
3 curry leaves
butter (knob of)
200ml fish stock
200ml coconut milk
250g tinned chopped tomatoes
500g vine tomatoes (chopped)
sugar and salt (to taste)
lime (juice of, to taste)

Method

For The Curried Tomatoes

Heat the oil and the onions slowly in a large, flat pan. When the onions begin to colour, add the garlic, chilli and ginger and cook for 2 minutes. Stir in the spices and curry leaves with the butter and cook for 2-3 minutes. Don't worry too much if it starts to 'catch'.

Add the liquids and tomatoes to the pan and continue to cook out on a lower heat for about 30 minutes, or until it thickens and starts to 'look like a curry'. Finish by adding salt and sugar and a squeeze of lime juice will help bring some life to it.

For The Monkfish

Preheat the oven to 180°C (fan).

Heat the oil in a pan until very hot. Carefully add the fish and cook on all sides until the fish has a nice colour. Pop it in the oven for 5-6 minutes. Don't worry if it is a little under cooked as you can finish it in the sauce.

Chef's Tip

As with most recipes, use your taste buds. Add more or less of any ingredient to suit your palate.

To Serve

Arrange the dish as you see fit. If you have any sauce left over, it's nice just on a piece of toast.

RASPBERRY BAKEWELL TART

SERVES 4

 *Dow's Vintage Port
(Portugal)*

Ingredients

Tart Base

1 pack 'all butter' puff pastry
4 heaped tsp raspberry jam

Tart Filling

400g butter (melted)
2 small eggs
175g pasteurised egg yolk
400g caster sugar
40g ground almonds

To Serve

ice cream or cream
fresh raspberries
shortbread (crumbled)

4 x 10cm x 3cm baking tins

Method

For The Tart Base

Divide the pastry into 4 and line each baking tin with the puff pastry. Place a dollop of raspberry jam in each base and leave to chill for half an hour in the fridge.

For The Tart Filling

Preheat the oven to 180°C (fan).

Mix all ingredients together in a large bowl over a *bain-marie* and whisk for about 3 minutes until it reaches a honey-like consistency. Pour the mix into the prepared tins and bake for 16 minutes, or until you have a golden colour and the wobble has gone. Leave to cool slightly.

To Serve

Turn out of the moulds, top with some fresh raspberries and serve just warm. Delicious with your favourite ice cream or just a good dollop of cream and crumbled shortbread.

Chef's Tip

This recipe can be altered all year round to suit seasonal fruits.

198
THE MAGPIE CAFE

14 Pier Road, Whitby, North Yorkshire, YO21 3PU

01947 602 058
www.magpiecafe.co.uk Twitter: @themagpiecafe

For nearly 80 years The Magpie Café has stood looking down on Whitby's picturesque working harbour. Situated in a 1750 building that was originally the home of a local merchant and which has served many functions over its 265 years, including being the pilotage where the pilots would wait to guide ships into the harbour and the offices of the Harrowing shipping company, finally becoming The Magpie in 1939.

Whilst probably best known for their fish and chips, first time visitors are frequently surprised to see the variety of dishes on offer. Naturally, fish and seafood are the main focus, considering the proximity of the fish market on the doorstep, however they do offer something for everyone.

It is not unusual to have a dozen varieties of fresh fish on offer from cod and haddock through to halibut and John Dory plus Whitby crab and lobster and, of course, the famous Whitby kipper.

Ian Robson and head chef Paul Gildroy, with their talented kitchen team, have received much critical acclaim over the years from food guides and journalists, most notably The Good Food Guide, with 36 years continuous entry, and the Hardens UK Restaurant Guide.

Friendly and efficient front of house service is overseen by Alison Slater and Duncan Robson whose grandparents and great grandparents respectively started the Magpie story.

There is an excellent wine list to complement the food and around 15 homemade desserts. The restaurant can seat 130 but as this is spread over a number of rooms, it never feels too big.

"As a family run restaurant we have always endeavoured to create an informal, relaxed setting and to offer great food at an affordable price."
Ian Robson

HADDOCK RAREBIT BONBONS

SERVES 4

*Domaine Perraud Mâcon-Villages
(France)*

Ingredients

Tomato And Fennel Sauce

1 bulb fennel (roughly chopped)
1 clove garlic (roughly chopped)
2 shallots (roughly chopped)
8 ripe tomatoes (quartered)
1 tbsp tomato purée
1 tbsp white wine vinegar
100ml vegetable stock
salt and pepper
rapeseed oil (for deep frying)

Haddock Rarebit Bonbons

200g haddock (skinned)
milk (for poaching)
1 heaped tbsp mashed potato
150g cheddar cheese (grated)
1 tbsp Henderson's relish
1 tsp grain mustard
Yorkshire bitter (splash of)
pepper (to season)
250g plain flour
cold water
breadcrumbs (to coat)

Garnish

salad leaves

Method

For The The Tomato And Fennel Sauce

Cook the fennel, garlic and shallots in a little oil until soft, without colouring.

Add the tomatoes, tomato purée, vinegar and stock. Bring to the boil and cook for around 20 minutes. Remove the pan from the heat and using a stick blender, blitz, keeping the sauce a little coarse.

Season with salt and pepper to taste and set aside on the stove top to keep warm.

For The Haddock Rarebit Bonbons

Poach the haddock in the milk. Strain and set aside to cool. Mix the fish with the potato, cheese, relish, mustard and bitter. Season with pepper only.

Mix the flour with cold water to form a batter with the consistency of single cream.

Form the haddock rarebit into 16 equal balls. Roll through the batter, then through the breadcrumbs. Repeat this so that the bonbons are double coated with the breadcrumbs.

Heat the oil to 180°C. Carefully add the bonbons and deep fry for 3-4 minutes, or until golden brown. Caution - never leave a pan of hot oil unattended. Remove from the oil and drain on kitchen paper.

Chef's Tip

Replace the haddock with sautéed leek for a vegetarian option.

To Serve

Spoon the sauce onto 4 warm plates and place 4 bonbons on each. Garnish with a few small salad leaves.

SEAFOOD PAELLA

SERVES 4

🍷 *Albariño Martín Códax, Galicia*
(Spain)

Ingredients

4 chicken thighs (boned, diced)
100g pancetta (diced)
100g chorizo (diced)
3 tbsp oil
1 onion (finely diced)
2 cloves garlic (crushed)
1 red pepper (diced)
1 green pepper (diced)
600g calasparra paella rice
250ml white wine
saffron (pinch of, add to the wine 30 minutes
prior to using)
1 tsp paprika
10 cherry tomatoes (cut in half)
1 litre chicken stock
200g salmon (diced into 8 pieces)
200g halibut (diced into 8 pieces)
8 king prawns
8 crevettes
8 king scallops
300g squid (cut into strips)
16 live mussels (washed, beards removed)
12 live clams (washed)
100g marsh samphire
salt and pepper
parsley (chopped, to sprinkle)

Method

For The Paella

Heat the oil in a paella pan or heavy bottomed sauté
pan. Add the chicken, pancetta and chorizo and cook until
well browned.

Add the onion, garlic and peppers and, once softened, add the
rice. Stir well before adding the wine, paprika and cherry
tomatoes. Bring to the boil.

Add the stock, bring back to the boil and place in the salmon,
halibut, prawns and crevettes. Cover the pan with a lid or foil
and reduce the heat. Cook for 8 minutes, remove the lid, add
the scallops, squid, mussels, clams and samphire, season with
salt and pepper.

Replace the lid and cook for 4-6 minutes, or until all the
mussels and clams have opened. Remove the pan from the heat,
sprinkle with chopped parsley and serve immediately.

Chef's Tip

Score the inner side of the squid in a crisscross so when it
cooks it curls and has a lovely diamond pattern.

To Serve

If you have used a large paella pan, simply place on the table
and let everyone dig in and enjoy.

BRIOCHE APPLE CHARLOTTE WITH BUTTERSCOTCH SAUCE

SERVES 6

 *Cazes Rivesaltes Ambré, Roussillon
(France)*

Ingredients

Brioche Apple Charlotte

300g Bramley apples (peeled, diced)
½ lemon (zest of)
1 tbsp granulated sugar
1 tsp water
300g Cox's apples (peeled, finely diced)
1 tsp vanilla extract (or seeds from 1 vanilla pod)
1 egg yolk
100g butter (softened)
8-10 slices brioche

Butterscotch Sauce

180g light brown soft sugar
907g tin golden syrup
100g butter
200ml double cream
1 tsp vanilla extract (or to taste)

To Serve

whipped cream

6 dariole moulds

Method

For The Brioche Apple Charlotte

Place the Bramley apples, lemon zest and sugar into a pan with a tablespoon of water and cook over a medium heat until the apples begin to fall. Remove the pan from the heat and stir in the diced Cox's apples, vanilla extract or seeds. Set aside to cool before stirring in the egg yolk.

Butter one side of the brioche and line the dariole moulds (buttered side against the mould). Spoon in the apple mix and top with brioche. Cover each pudding with tin foil, then cover the puddings with a tray and place a weight on top. Press the puddings for 1 hour.

Preheat the oven to 200°C. Remove the tray and bake the puddings for 30 minutes. Remove from the oven and carefully turn the puddings out onto the tray. Place back into the oven for a further 10 minutes, or until golden in colour.

Chef's Tip

You can prevent the apples from browning by soaking the pieces in a bowl of cold water and lemon juice. You should use a ratio of 1 tablespoon of lemon juice to 1 cup of water. You only need to soak the apple for 3-5 minutes, before draining and rinsing.

For The Butterscotch Sauce

Place the sugar, syrup and butter into a pan. Bring to the boil and boil rapidly for 3 minutes. Remove from the heat and cool slightly before stirring in the cream and vanilla.

To Serve

Serve the puddings hot or cold with a generous serving of butterscotch sauce and whipped cream.

208
THE PIPE
& GLASS INN

West End, South Dalton, Beverley, East Yorkshire, HU17 7PN

01430 810 246
www.pipeandglass.co.uk

There are many reasons why The Pipe and Glass Inn at South Dalton holds a coveted Michelin star.

Guests receive a warm welcome from James and Kate Mackenzie and team (he's the chef; she runs front of house), the atmosphere is inviting, unpretentious and relaxed; cool and airy in the summer, yet cosy and cocooning in colder weather. The real star of the show, of course, is the food, which has the top restaurant critics drooling. Jay Rayner in The Observer called The Pipe a 'class act... there was no doubting the quality of the cookery', while The Independent's Christopher Hirst praised the 'inventive Mackenzie' for 'ingenious dishes' and for 'not forgetting that he's running a pub'.

The bar has kept a country pub feel, with a conservatory looking out over the garden that has a spectacular long table for up to 28 people. Herbs and vegetables often travel just yards to the restaurant, as they are sourced from these fantastic kitchen gardens.

Guests looking for something extra special can book the conservatory for parties of more than 20 or, even more exclusively, the Pipe's first-floor private dining room, the Hotham Room, for between six and ten people. For really luxurious overnight accommodation, there are the Pipe's five boutique suites, offering comfort and glamour.

Set in the glorious surroundings of the Hotham Estate, The Pipe and Glass holds East Yorkshire's first and only Michelin star and the Good Pub Guide's National Dining Pub of the Year 2015.

VENISON TARTARE WITH HAGGIS SCOTCH EGG, DAMSON, JUNIPER & SLOE GIN JAM

SERVES 4

Barolo
(Italy)

Ingredients

Damson Jam

1kg damsons
250g caster sugar
200ml water
crushed juniper berries (large pinch of)
2 measures sloe gin

Venison Tartare

300g venison loin (trimmed)
1 shallot (finely diced)
30g cornichons (finely diced)
30g baby capers
3 drops Tabasco
2 dashes Worcester sauce
2 tsp rapeseed mayonnaise
2 tsp rapeseed oil
2 tbsp parsley (finely chopped)
salt and pepper (to taste)
crushed juniper berries (pinch of)

Haggis Scotch Egg

150g haggis
100g sausage meat
crushed juniper berries (pinch of)
salt and pepper
4 quail eggs
plain flour (to dust)
1 egg (beaten)
breadcrumbs (to cover)

Garnish

pickled and fresh radish
green herbs

4 cooks' rings (optional)

Method

For The Damson Jam

Place all the ingredients into a saucepan and cook over a medium heat until the damsons have broken down. Remove from the heat, pass through a fine sieve and allow to cool. When cool, the jam should be a thick sauce consistency.

Chef's Tip

This will make more damson jam than is required, however it keeps well and is delicious with cold meats.

For The Venison Tartare

Place the venison in the freezer until firm, then chop into small cubes. Combine the shallot, cornichons and baby capers, then stir into the venison cubes. Add 3 drops of Tabasco and 2 dashes of Worcester sauce, the mayonnaise, oil and parsley and mix again. Add salt, pepper and juniper to taste. Add more Tabasco if you like it to have a kick. Push the mix into individual rings and press out, or place into one serving bowl to share.

For The Haggis Scotch Egg

Mix the haggis, sausage meat and crushed juniper berries in a bowl. Season well and put to one side. Boil the quail eggs for 2½ minutes. Cool in iced water and peel. Dust the eggs with flour to help the sausage meat stick to them. Flatten a quarter of the haggis mix on the palm of your hand and wrap around an egg. Repeat. Pass the eggs through flour and beaten egg, then roll in breadcrumbs until covered. Deep fry at 190°C for about 2½ minutes. Leave to rest before serving.

To Serve

Serve as pictured.

BAKED HALIBUT WITH COBNUT CRUST, CAULIFLOWER & COCKLES

SERVES 4

 Chablis (France)
Or any good white Burgundy

Ingredients

4 x 200g chunky portions halibut or cod
400ml fish stock

Cauliflower Champ

1 cauliflower
200ml whipping cream
100ml water
1 bunch spring onions (finely sliced)
salt and white pepper

Cauliflower Garnish

Romanesque cauliflower
yellow cauliflower
purple cauliflower
butter (knob of)
saffron (pinch of, optional)
white wine vinegar (to pickle)

Cobnut Crust

100g cobnuts or hazelnuts (roughly chopped)
100g breadcrumbs
40g Parmesan cheese (grated)
50g butter (melted)
1 tbsp chives (chopped)

Cockle Sauce

1kg fresh cockles
200ml white wine
1 shallot (sliced)
1 bunch dill (chopped)
150ml double cream

Garnish

150g cobnuts or hazelnuts (toasted, chopped)

Method

To Make The Cauliflower Champ

Thinly slice the white cauliflower florets and place in a saucepan with the cream and water. Cover and cook on a medium heat until the cauliflower is just cooked, about 20 minutes. Remove from the heat and blend to a smooth purée in a food processor. Season with white pepper and salt to taste. Reserve until needed.

For The Cauliflower Garnishes

Boil the Romanesque in salted water until just tender and finish with a little butter.

Cook the yellow cauliflower with some saffron added to the water.

To give a contrast to the dish, simply thinly slice the purple cauliflower and place in some white wine vinegar to pickle for 2 minutes.

To Make The Cobnut Crust

Mix all the ingredients together in a bowl with your hand to form a rough crumb.

For The Halibut

Preheat the oven to 180°C (fan).

Place the halibut fillets into a deep baking tray and top each one with the cobnut crust. Pour the stock around the fish and place in the oven for 8-12 minutes, dependent on the size and thickness of the fish. Remove from the oven, the crust should be golden brown.

> **Chef's Tip**
> Try to use nice, thick pieces of fish.

For The Cockle Sauce

Heat a large saucepan, place in the cockles, shallot and wine. Cover and cook over a high heat until the cockles open. Remove the cooked cockles, pick the meat out of them and reserve. Pour the cream into the cockle cooking stock and reduce until a sauce consistency. Add the cockle meat back to the sauce to warm through. Finish with the dill.

To Serve

Add the spring onions to the cauliflower purée and warm through. Place a large spoonful of the champ on each plate, arrange the coloured cauliflower and set the fish on top. Spoon the cockle sauce around and garnish with the toasted nuts.

BAKED DARK CHOCOLATE 'MILLIONAIRE' PUDDING

SERVES 4

 Banyuls
(France)

Ingredients

Chocolate Pudding

250g dark chocolate
125g sugar
2 eggs
125g butter
50g cocoa powder
40g plain flour
1 tbsp cornflour

Shortbread

100g butter
50g caster sugar
100g plain flour
50g cornflour
salt (pinch of)
½ vanilla pod (seeds of)

Filling

1 tin Carnation caramel

To Serve

200g cinder toffee ice cream
sea salt flakes (to sprinkle)
cocoa powder (to dust)

4 ramekins or 1 large dish

Method

For The Shortbread

Place all the ingredients in a mixer and combine well to form a dough. Wrap in cling film, rest for at least 30 minutes.

Preheat the oven to 180°C (fan).

Roll the dough on a lightly floured surface to 1cm thick. Place on a non-stick baking sheet and bake for 6-10 minutes. Leave to cool.

For The Chocolate Pudding

Whisk the sugar and eggs together until fluffy and white. Melt the chocolate and butter together over a *bain-marie* or in a microwave. Once melted, add the chocolate mix to the egg mix and whisk together.

Gently fold the dry ingredients into the chocolate mixture. Spoon the mixture into individual ramekin dishes or an ovenproof dish and put to one side.

Chef's Tip

Use a good quality dark chocolate.

To Serve

Preheat the oven to 180°C (fan).

Bake the chocolate mixture for 5-10 minutes, depending on the size of the dish you are using. The pudding should be soft in the middle and crusty on the surface.

Place the Carnation caramel into a squeezy sauce bottle. Inject a little caramel into the cooked pudding to create little pockets of runny caramel inside the warm pudding. Dust with cocoa powder.

Break the biscuits over the top of the pudding to give a crunchy topping. Serve with a scoop of cinder toffee ice cream topped with a little more caramel sauce and a pinch of sea salt flakes.

218
THE ROSE & CROWN
AT ROMALDKIRK

Barnard Castle, Co Durham, DL12 9EB

01833 650 213
www.rose-and-crown.co.uk

The Rose and Crown is an 18th Century inn standing on the green of the picture postcard village of Romaldkirk in Teesdale, the most southerly of the Durham Dales, near to the market town of Barnard Castle.

Their approach is to combine the traditional charm of this historic building with contemporary touches and an ambience of comfort and relaxation. At the heart of what they do is great food and drink that reflects the location and served with a smile.

The menu is influenced by the seasons and ingredients local to the area. Head chef, Dave Hunter, is himself born and raised in Teesdale so has a great enthusiasm for the region and for showcasing what it can offer on a plate.

He is passionate about good food and with the help of his dedicated team he creates dishes that taste great, satisfy the appetite and show imagination and flair. The Rose and Crown has been recognised with 2 AA Rosettes and Taste Durham Highest Quality Assured and Local Champion accolades.

There is an excellent selection of over 60 wines from both the New and Old World as well as local real ales, continental lagers, 15 malt whiskies, including a strong showing from Islay, and a good selection of gins, including Durham Gin which is distilled in the county.

"Having been born and raised in Teesdale, my philosophy is to use the very best of local ingredients. My butcher, Joe Simpson, is only eight miles away in Cockfield - he raises, slaughters and hangs much of our meat."
Head chef, Dave Hunter.

GROUSE LIVER PARFAIT WITH CUMBERLAND SAUCE

SERVES 5

 Pinotage Kleinkloof Paarl, 2011
(South Africa)

Ingredients

Grouse Liver Parfait

250g grouse livers (cleaned)
3 egg yolks
210g butter (melted)
100ml double cream
1 shot port
½ tsp salt and pepper
1 tsp redcurrant jelly
nutmeg and cayenne pepper (pinch of)

Cumberland Sauce

1 orange
1 lemon
220g redcurrant jelly
1 tsp Dijon mustard
5 tbsp ruby port
1 tsp ground ginger
black pepper (pinch of)
salt (pinch of)

Toasted Mixed Seeds

250g mixed seeds (sunflower, pumpkin, sesame)
50ml maple syrup

To Garnish And Serve

blueberries
nasturtium leaves
Melba toast
salad

terrine mould

Method

For The Grouse Liver Parfait

Preheat the oven to 160°C (fan).

Place all the ingredients, except the butter, into a blender and blitz until smooth.

Slowly add the melted butter until combined and *emulsified*. Pass through a sieve into a terrine mould.

Cook in a *bain-marie* in the oven for 45-55 minutes until the centre is over 70°C. Leave to cool.

For The Cumberland Sauce

Put a saucepan of water on to boil. Pare the zest of the orange and lemon, taking as little of the white pith as possible, then cut into long, fine shreds (*julienne*). Drop into the boiling water and leave to simmer for 5 minutes to soften and remove any bitterness, then drain.

Place the redcurrant jelly, mustard and port into a saucepan and stir, then whisk over a low heat until smoothly amalgamated. Bring up to the boil, add the *blanched* orange and lemon zest, the ginger and a little salt and freshly ground black pepper. Simmer gently for 5 minutes then pour into a serving jug or bowl. Leave to cool.

For The Toasted Mixed Seeds

Preheat the oven to 180°C (fan).

Coat the seeds with the maple syrup and bake for 10 minutes.

To Serve

Serve as pictured with Melba toast and your favourite salad.

> **Chef's Tip**
> Use a warm knife to cut the parfait.

TRIO OF JOE SIMPSON'S HERDWICK MUTTON WITH PAN HAGGERTY

SERVES 6

Shiraz Viognier, Hangin' Snakes, Langmeil, 2011 (Australia)

Ingredients

Braised Shoulder Of Mutton

2½kg shoulder of mutton (on the bone)
1 large bunch rosemary (leaves picked, finely chopped)
1 unwaxed lemon (zest of)
freshly ground black pepper (to taste)
8 banana shallots (peeled, halved lengthways)
2 whole bulbs garlic (peeled, halved)
750ml red wine

Mutton Loin And Sausages

1 mutton loin (trimmed of all fat and sinew)
oil (drizzle of)
3 mutton sausages

Pan Haggerty

1 tbsp vegetable oil
250g streaky bacon
6 potatoes (thinly sliced into rounds)
2 onions (peeled, sliced)
150g Cotherstone cheese (plus extra to finish, grated)
salt and freshly ground black pepper (to taste)

To Serve

baby seasonal vegetables

Method

For The Braised Shoulder Of Mutton (Prepare in advance)
Preheat the oven to 140°C (fan).
Rub the rosemary, lemon zest and black pepper all over the top of the mutton. Put the shallots and garlic in a deep roasting tray and add any remaining herb stalks.
Lay the mutton on top and pour in the wine; the liquid should just be touching the bottom of the meat - if not, top up with water.
Seal the top of the roasting tray with a layer of baking parchment followed by foil. Place in the oven for at least 6 hours or until the mutton is cooked.
Remove the foil and lift out. When cool enough to handle, pull all the meat away from the bone and place in bowl.
Strain the juices, discarding the garlic and shallots. Reduce slightly in an uncovered saucepan over a medium heat. Add a little of the jus to the meat and mix well. Season and roll up in cling film like a Christmas cracker and tie the ends. Refrigerate for 2 hours. Cut into rounds for service. Reserve the rest of the jus for the finished dish.

For The Pan Haggerty (Prepare in advance)
Preheat the oven to 180°C (fan).
Heat the vegetable oil in a deep, ovenproof pan. Fry the bacon for 3-4 minutes, or until golden-brown and slightly crisp. Remove from the pan and set aside to drain on kitchen paper.
In the same pan, arrange a layer of potatoes in the bottom. Cover the potatoes with a layer of onions. Layer over some crisp bacon and cheese, then season with salt and freshly ground black pepper. Repeat the process finishing with a layer of potatoes on top. Season well.
Cover with foil and bake for 30-40 minutes until tender. Chill, then cut to desired shape.

For The Mutton Loin, Sausages And To Serve
Preheat the oven to 140°C (fan).
Seal the loin in a little oil in a hot pan until browned all over. Transfer to an oven tray. Seal the sausages and shoulder slices in the same pan, transferring onto the oven tray when ready.
Place in the oven for 7 minutes, then leave to rest.
Sprinkle some extra cheese on top of the pan haggerty. Add to the oven tray with the mutton and cook for 7 minutes. Slice the mutton loin and sausages, warm the jus and plate all elements as pictured. Serve with baby vegetables.

> **Chef's Tip**
> Ask your butcher to remove the fat and sinew from the mutton loin.

WARM CHOCOLATE FONDANT

SERVES 4

🍷 *Black Noble, De Bortoli*
(Austrailia)

Method

To Prepare The Ramekins

Brush the moulds with melted butter and dust with cocoa powder.

For The Warm Chocolate Fondant

Preheat the oven to 180°C (fan).

Mix together the eggs, egg yolks and sugar. Melt the chocolate and butter together over a pan of slightly simmering water (*bain-marie*). Once melted, mix with the egg mixture. Fold in the flour and cocoa powder.

Pipe the mixture into the prepared ramekins and bake for 11 minutes.

> **Chef's Tip**
> Use the best quality chocolate you can afford.

To Serve

Turn the fondants out onto a plate and serve with vanilla ice cream and fresh, seasonal berries.

Ingredients

Chocolate Fondant

3 medium eggs
3 egg yolks
150g caster sugar
120g 70% dark chocolate
150g butter (plus extra for lining moulds)
60g plain flour
20g cocoa powder (plus extra for lining moulds)

To Serve

vanilla ice cream
fresh, seasonal berries
raspberry purée

4 ramekins

228
SALTWATER FISH COMPANY

Fenwick Food Hall, Northumberland Street, Newcastle, NE1 7AS

0191 239 6613
www.saltwaterfish.co.uk Twitter: @_saltwater_fish

Saltwater Fish Company is a new, stylish seafood bar and fishmonger that showcases the best seasonal catches of the day in a lively dining environment.

Chef and North East restaurateur Terry Laybourne has expanded his 21 Hospitality Group with the opening of this buzzy seafood bar within the spectacular new food hall of Newcastle's biggest department store, Fenwick.

For Terry, the move reflects a return to his roots with fish and seafood, which is where he built his reputation upon returning to Newcastle in the 1980s.

Saltwater offers fast, casual, seafood dining; there is counter seating for 20, an open kitchen, creative chefs and knowledgeable service staff. A blackboard menu highlights the seasonal, daily specials, altering throughout the day.

Menu choices change with the seasons and might include freshly prepared fish, oysters from different beds, French-style fruits de mer platters, salt and pepper squid, seafood cocktail, crab sandwiches and salads. A fish focussed wine list accompanies the menu.

Chefs are working hand in hand with the fishmonger, taking a 'we cook what we sell, we sell what we cook' approach.

Fish is being cooked at the counter ensuring a lively environment. Chefs treat the fish lightly, grilling or steaming, showcasing their natural flavours. The emphasis is on the great seafood that comes from the fabulous larder off the North East coastline as well as other ports around the UK.

Diners have the rare opportunity to see and discuss how seafood is prepared and cooked. The experienced kitchen team are happy to show how to get the most out of fresh fish.

Saltwater is open seven days a week, 11am-8pm Monday to Saturday; 11am-4pm Sunday. There is a daily 'Oyster Happy Hour' from 3pm-5pm offering favourably priced oysters and fizz.

Saltwater Fish Company is a stylish, seafood bar and fishmonger; an oasis within a buzzy Fenwick Food Hall. A blackboard menu showcases the seasonal and daily catches from the fabulous larder off the North East and UK coastline.

SALTWATER
FISH COMPANY

PROVENCAL FISH SOUP

SERVES 4

 Picpoul de Pinet, Hugues de Beauvignac 2014
Coteaux du Languedoc (France)

Ingredients

Fish Soup

85ml extra virgin olive oil
75g onions (finely chopped)
75g celery (finely chopped)
75g leek (finely chopped)
75g fennel (finely chopped)
3 cloves garlic (peeled, finely chopped)
40g tomato paste
orange zest (grated, pinch of)
1 red pepper (seeded, chopped)
2 fresh bay leaves
1 sprig thyme
saffron (large pinch of)
200g tinned tomatoes (chopped)
½ orange (juice of)
600ml fish stock
100g shellfish (langoustine shells, velvet crabs,
langoustine shells or Atlantic prawns, rinsed,
coarsely chopped)
900g mixed fish (small red mullets, gurnards,
monkfish etc, cleaned, cut into chunks)
cayenne pepper (large pinch of)
salt and pepper

To Serve

garlic croutons
Gruyère cheese (grated)
rouille (olive oil, breadcrumbs, garlic, saffron
and chillies)

Method

For The Fish Soup

Heat the oil in a large, shallow pan. Add the chopped vegetables and garlic and sweat slowly for 20 minutes. Stir in the tomato paste, orange zest, red pepper, bay, thyme, saffron and shellfish.

Cook for 3-4 minutes, then add the chopped tomatoes, orange juice and half of the fish stock.

Bring to a simmer and cook for 5-10 minutes before adding the fish.

Simmer for a further 5 minutes then liquidise, seasoning with cayenne, salt and pepper.

Force through a fine sieve then thin with remaining fish stock .

Check the seasoning and adjust if necessary.

To Serve

Serve piping hot with lots of garlic croutons, rouille and grated Gruyère cheese.

SEARED TUNA WITH GARLIC, CHILLI & HERBS

SERVES 4

🍷 *Muscadet Sevre-et-Maine Sur Lie Carte d'Or,*
Sauvion et Fils 2014 Pays Nantais, Loire Valley (France)

Method

For The Dressing

Stir all the ingredients together. Check the balance of flavours.

For The Fennel Salad (Optional)

Shave the fennel and celery very finely on a mandolin. Season with the lemon juice, olive oil and sea salt.

For The Tuna

Sear the tuna in hot olive oil for 3 minutes, flipping the fish at the last moment. Season with a little lemon juice and sea salt.

To Serve

Spoon the dressing over and around the tuna. Serve with the fennel salad on the side (optional).

Ingredients

Tuna

4 x 160g sashimi grade tuna steaks
1 tbsp olive oil
lemon juice (spritz of)
salt

Dressing

3 tbsp parsley (chopped)
1 tbsp oregano (chopped)
1 red chilli (very finely chopped)
3 cloves garlic (finely chopped)
½ lemon (juice and zest of)
2 tbsp salted anchovies (chopped)
2 tbsp Cabernet Sauvignon vinegar
5 tbsp best quality extra virgin olive oil

Fennel Salad (Optional)

1 bulb fennel
2 sticks celery (peeled)
lemon juice (spritz of)
extra virgin olive oil
fine sea salt

BITTER CHOCOLATE MOUSSE

SERVES 4

Ingredients

Bitter Chocolate Mousse

133g chocolate couverture (67% cocoa butter)
2 leaves gelatine (softened)
100ml full-fat milk
200ml whipping cream (chilled)

Garnish

white and dark chocolate (shaved)

Method

For The The Bitter Chocolate Mousse

Place the chocolate into a stainless steel bowl.

Bring a small pan of water to the boil, remove from the heat and sit the bowl of chocolate on top to melt slowly.

Whisk the cream until thickened and semi-whipped.

Bring the milk to the boil, then remove from the heat. Squeeze any excess moisture from the gelatine, then add it to the milk. Stir to dissolve.

Pour the milk mixture over the melted chocolate. Stir until smooth and glossy.

Remove from the heat and allow to cool to about 35-40°C, then fold in the semi-whipped cream.

Transfer to a Pyrex dish and refrigerate for 4 hours or so.

To Serve

Dip a large metal spoon in heated water and use to carve a large *quenelle* from the chocolate mousse. Transfer to a serving plate and garnish with shaved white and dark chocolate and serve as pictured.

238
SHIBDEN MILL INN

Shibden Mill Fold, Shibden, Halifax, West Yorkshire, HX3 7UL

01422 365 840
www.shibdenmillinn.com Twitter: twitter.com/shibdenmill

The 5 star, 17th Century Shibden Mill Inn serves double AA Rosette winning dishes deep in the rolling countryside of West Yorkshire's historic Shibden Valley.

This family-owned property presents 11 lovingly and individually styled rooms, a cosy bar and dining area with low beamed ceilings and open fires, a lavish grill room and a wine loft for private dining. The Inn's reputation for award-winning food and warm hospitality extends far beyond Yorkshire's borders.

Darren Parkinson is a dynamic head chef with an eye for excellence and innovative food combinations. His culinary team attracts widespread acclaim for shaping dishes rich with inspiration, quality and diversity. The menu is based on the seasons – using the very best produce available at any given time from their own garden or close network of local suppliers. It proudly showcases the region's finest fish, poultry, game, meat, vegetables and fruit. A wide selection of Cask Marque-accredited ales, including the Shibden Mill's own brew, and an extensive wine list have been designed to complement Darren's menu.

This multi award-winning Inn continues to impress and was recently crowned Great British Pub of the Year 2015 by Sky.

Our family-owned 17th Century Inn offers 5 star accommodation, 2 AA Rosette dining and warm Yorkshire hospitality in an historic country setting. Both the cosy à la carte and lavish grill room offerings showcase the best, seasonal, locally sourced produce.

HANDPICKED WHITBY CRAB & CHICKEN SKIN SANDWICH, WARM CRAB STICK, SPINACH & WATERCRESS RISOTTO

SERVES 4

 Chablis Vieilles Vignes, Tour du Roy, Domaine des Malandes (France)

Ingredients

Crab

1 whole dressed Whitby crab
20ml rice wine vinegar
2 shallots (chopped)
10g chives (finely chopped)
5g lemon and orange zest (grated)
20g mayonnaise

Spinach And Watercress Risotto

50g watercress (*blanched*)
50g spinach (*blanched*)
200g vialone rice
100ml water
10ml Yorkshire rapeseed oil
1 large shallot (chopped)
400ml dry white wine
50g Parmesan
salt and pepper

Crispy Chicken Skin

100g chicken breast skin
salt

Warm Crab Stick

1 sheet pre-rolled puff pastry
1 egg (beaten)
50g brown crab meat
10g chives (chopped)
salt and pepper

Baby Vegetables

4 baby leeks or spring onions
4 baby carrots (peeled)
4 breakfast radishes
5 spears asparagus
10ml Yorkshire rapeseed oil

Method

For The Crab

Empty the shell meat into a bowl and run your fingers through the meat to check for any loose crab shell. Reduce the wine vinegar with the shallots until evaporated. Cool to room temperature. Mix all the ingredients together, season and chill in the fridge.

For The Spinach And Watercress Risotto

Blitz the watercress, spinach and water in a food processor for 60 seconds. Place in the fridge.

Cook the rice with the oil, shallots and wine until translucent.

Just before serving, mix the spinach and watercress water into the risotto, turn the heat down to low and season with the cheese, salt and pepper.

> **Chef's Tip**
> Using a good quality risotto grain will absorb more liquid therefore carrying more flavour without over cooking.

For The Crispy Chicken Skin

Preheat the oven to 160°C (fan).

Place the skin between 2 flat baking trays lined with wax paper and bake for 1 hour. Season with salt and cut into squares with a sharp knife.

For The Warm Crab Stick

Cut the pastry into a 15cm square and chill in the fridge.

Season the crab meat, mix in the chives and place in a plastic piping bag. Pipe 3 or 4 lines of crab down 1 side of the pastry. Brush the egg on the other side and fold the pastry over on top of the crab, pressing down in between the crab. Freeze for 2 hours.

Preheat the oven to 175°C (fan).

Slice across the pastry to form sticks. Bake for 12 minutes.

For The Baby Vegetables

Blanch the baby leeks for 1 minute in salted water followed by 2 minutes for the carrots. Slice the radishes finely and use a potato peeler to peel fine slices from the raw asparagus.

To Serve

Sandwich the crab between the crispy chicken skin, gently warm the vegetables in the rapeseed oil and serve as pictured.

ROASTED LAMB RUMP, POMMES ANNA, ELDERBERRIES, FIGS, BARLEY, PICKLED SHALLOT & DENHOLME GATE HONEY

SERVES 4

🍷 *Rioja Reserva, Tempranillo, Bodegas El Meson (Spain)*

Ingredients

4 x 180g lamb rumps

Barley

10g pearl barley
rapeseed oil

Pommes Anna

2 large Albert Bartlett potatoes (peeled)
100g *clarified butter*
1 sprig thyme (picked)

Pickled Shallot

1 large shallot (peeled)
50g sugar
50ml white wine vinegar
50ml water
1 clove garlic
1 sprig thyme
1 sprig rosemary
1 star anise

Elderberries

20g cornflour
20g plain flour
50ml sparkling water
4 freshly cut elderberry sprigs

Figs

2 large figs (halved)
4 tbsp Denholme Gate honey

4 ramekins

Method

For The Barley (Prepare the day before)

Boil the barley for 20 minutes and leave to dry overnight at room temperature.

When you are ready to serve, fry the barley in the rapeseed oil for 3-4 minutes and season with salt.

For The Pommes Anna

Preheat the oven to 180°C (fan).

Cut the potatoes into cylinders, then finely slice into discs and mix with the *clarified butter*. Stack the potato slices in the ramekins, cover and place in a ramekin. Cover with the remaining butter, sprinkle with the picked thyme and cook in the oven for 25 minutes.

For The Lamb Rump

Preheat the oven to 190°C (fan).

Slowly fry the rumps in a pan, skin-side down, until coloured. Turn the lamb over and colour the other side.

Place into the oven for 8 minutes, remove and leave to rest for 10 minutes.

> **Chef's Tip**
> Buy the lamb rump from a good, local butcher. Rest the meat after cooking for at least 10 minutes. You can add some spice to the meat by marinating it overnight in oil and dried chilli.

For The Pickled Shallot

Slice the shallot into 10mm rings and remove the centres.

Bring the remaining ingredients to the boil, then set aside to cool for 10 minutes. Place the raw shallot rings into the liquor to pickle for a few minutes.

For The Elderberries

Combine the flours and water to form a batter. Dip the heads of the elderberries into the batter and shallow fry for 30 seconds. Serve immediately.

To Serve

Spoon a little honey onto each fig half and bake for 2 minutes. Slice the lamb into 3 and place in the middle of the plate with the pommes Anna. Arrange the figs, barley and shallots on and around the lamb and drizzle with honey.

LEMON & PASSION FRUIT TART, COCONUT WAFERS, PASSION FRUIT PUREE

SERVES 4

🍷 *Riesling, Noble Late Harvest, Mellifera,
Jordan Estate (South Africa)*

Ingredients

Coconut Wafers

25g butter
20g glucose syrup
40g caster sugar
15g plain flour
15g desiccated coconut

Pastry

30g cornflour
250g plain flour
85g caster sugar (little extra for caramelising)
90g butter
2 medium, free range eggs
2 tbsp lemon and lime zest (grated)

Lemon And Passion Fruit Custard

150ml double cream
200g caster sugar
3 medium, free range eggs
50ml lemon juice
50ml passion fruit purée

Passion Fruit Purée

100ml passion fruit juice
2g agar agar
100g caster sugar

To Serve

2 passion fruit
sugar (to sprinkle)

4 x 8cm tart cases

Method

For The Coconut Wafers

Melt all the ingredients together until well combined. Leave to set in the fridge for 2 hours in a square, plastic container.

Preheat the oven to 180°C (fan).

When set, place the mixture on a silicone mat and cook for 7-8 minutes until golden brown. Cut into desired shapes with a sharp knife.

For The Pastry

Preheat the oven to 175°C (fan).

Mix all the ingredients in a large bowl or Kitchen Aid until combined. Place on a floured surface, roll out and line the tart cases. Blind bake for 14 minutes. Leave to cool.

For The Lemon And Passion Fruit Custard

Whisk all the ingredients together and leave to rest at room temperature for an hour.

Preheat the oven to 105°C (fan).

Fill the tart cases with the custard and bake for 20 minutes until firm.

> **Chef's Tip**
>
> Cook the pastry case a good few hours before setting the custard. Use a brûlée torch to dissipate any bubbles on the surface of the custard just before cooking in the cases.

For The Passion Fruit Purée

Boil the juice with the sugar, then add the agar agar. Set in the fridge for 1 hour. Blitz in a food processor, then put in a squeezy bottle.

To Serve

Serve the tarts at room temperature. Cover with a little sugar and caramelise with a blow torch. Halve the passion fruit and caramelise the centre with a little more sugar. Serve as pictured.

248
WENSLEYDALE HEIFER

Main Street, West Witton, Leyburn, Yorkshire DL8 4LS

01969 622 322
www.wensleydaleheifer.co.uk Twitter: @WensleyHeifer

The Wensleydale Heifer is Yorkshire's first boutique hotel situated between Leyburn and Hawes in the heart of The Yorkshire Dales, known as one of the most beautiful counties in the country. The AA 5 star restaurant, with rooms celebrated for their quirkiness and charm, has attracted guests from near and far. The Heifer is a joint venture between David and Lewis Moss, father and son. David, patron/chef along with head chef Craig Keenan have created the Heifer's stunning dishes that have delighted and impressed customers and national food critics alike, ensuring their continued prominent entries in The Michelin Guide and Good Food Guide.

The philosophy in the kitchen is 'keep it simple'; source the best quality ingredients, cook them well and let the natural flavours speak for themselves. Diners can enjoy the finest fish and seafood that the British Isles has to offer and superb local meats, vegetables and cheeses.

The Heifer offers a wide variety of differing menus, including their seafood menu, a dedicated steak and early bird fixed price menu available at lunch and dinner. Alternatively for a light lunchtime snack, choose from the comprehensive tapas and unique sandwich menus.

Experience the Sunday lunch that a renowned food critic described as 'one of the best in Yorkshire'.

The restaurant is contemporary decadence, with its chocolate leather chairs, linen table cloths and Doug Hyde artwork; great for an evening out or celebrating a special occasion. The Fish Bar, with its wooden block tables and rattan chairs, is perfect for a less formal dining experience. Guests can also enjoy the fine weather in the restaurant garden.

If guests need a rest after overindulging or simply want a relaxing weekend away or a short break, the Wensleydale Heifer has 13 luxurious rooms, each with its own unique theme and all the charm of a 17th Century inn.

The lounge with a roaring fire and soft leather furnishings is the perfect spot to relax.

Our dedicated team of chefs -
David Moss at front, Craig Keenan,
Graeme Moss, Kristin Thompson,
James Knights, Sam Hammond, Dan King
and Michal Wiater.

SWEET CHILLI KING PRAWNS

SERVES 4

 Gewurztraminer Hugel & Fils
(France)

Ingredients

Prawns

16 tiger king prawns (shelled, de-veined)
100ml cold water
200g plain flour (seasoned)

Sweet Chilli Sauce

1kg caster sugar
½ litre cold water
100g glucose syrup
100ml white wine vinegar
4 red chillies (roughly chopped)
2 sticks lemongrass (roughly chopped)
50g fresh ginger (peeled, roughly chopped)
4 cloves garlic (peeled, roughly chopped)
10g fresh basil
10g fresh coriander
100ml sriracha
10g sesame seeds
10g black sesame seeds

Garnish

20g toasted coconut
20g cashew nuts
10g micro coriander

Method

For The Sweet Chilli Sauce

Combine the sugar, water and glucose in a large heavy bottomed saucepan. Place on a high heat and bring to a golden caramel. Add the vinegar, taking care as it will bubble and spit and the caramel will be extremely hot! Pour the hot caramel onto the chilli, ginger, garlic, lemongrass and fresh herbs. Leave to cool. When completely cool, blend in a food processor, then add the sriracha sauce. Transfer to a bowl and sprinkle in the sesame seeds.

For The Prawns

Place the prawns into the flour, remove, dip into the water, then back into the flour. See the chef's tip.

Deep fry at 190ºC for 4-5 minutes. Drain on kitchen paper. Pick up the prawns by the tail, taking care as they will be quite hot, and dip them into the sweet chilli sauce.

Chef's Tip

For the perfect light batter dip the prawns in seasoned flour, then in water, then back into the seasoned flour. This creates a fantastic, crunchy batter and also works with many different products.

To Serve

Garnish the plate with toasted coconut and cashew nuts. Place the dipped prawns on the nut mix. Finish off with a drizzle of sweet chilli sauce. and garnish with the micro coriander.

MAPLE ROAST LOBSTER, KING PRAWN & SCALLOP SALAD

SERVES 4

Eins-Zwei-Dry Riesling
(Germany)

Ingredients

Lobster, Scallops, Prawns And Bacon

300g smoked back bacon
8 fresh king scallops (roe removed)
12 tiger king prawns (shelled, de-veined)
200g lobster meat (cooked)
200g maple syrup
20g unsalted butter
olive oil (splash of)
1 lemon (juice of)

Croutons

1 small ciabatta loaf
olive oil
salt and pepper

Salad

400g gem lettuce hearts
40g sun blushed tomatoes
20g cucumber (thinly sliced)

Garnish

crispy, fried shallots

Method

For The Croutons

Preheat the oven to 200°C.

Dice the ciabatta into 5cm squares, toss in olive oil and season. Bake for 8-10 minutes until crisp. Place to one side.

For The Lobster, Scallops, Prawns And Bacon

Cook the smoked bacon until crisp. When cooled, shred into thin strips. Put to one side.

Remove the roe from the scallops, then cut them in half from side to side.

Heat a little olive oil in a large frying pan over a high heat.

Sear the prawns and scallops on each side until golden. Add the butter and turn the heat down to medium. Toss in the cooked lobster meat and bacon, giving a good toss to mix together. Pour in the maple syrup and lemon juice. Give another toss to ensure everything is glazed in the syrup.

Chef's Tip

When cooking live lobster, place them in the freezer for 2 minutes before cooking. This puts the lobster to sleep and makes the process much more humane.

To Serve

Wash the gem lettuce hearts in cold water, separating the leaves and discarding any large, outside, dark leaves as these can be bitter. Place the gem leaves, sliced cucumber, sun blushed tomatoes and croutons into a large bowl.

Add the maple glazed shellfish and bacon, give a good toss and place into a serving dish.

Garnish with a few crispy, fried shallots.

COCONUT PANNA COTTA, COCONUT LOLLIES, PIÑA COLADA

SERVES 4

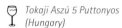 Tokaji Aszú 5 Puttonyos
(Hungary)

Ingredients

Coconut Panna Cotta

2 x 400ml cans coconut milk
400ml full-fat milk
100g sugar
1 vanilla pod
8 leaves gelatine (soaked in cold water)

Coconut Lollies

small tub coconut ice cream
200g good quality white chocolate
200g desiccated coconut

Piña Colada (Makes 800ml)

2 shots Malibu
50g fresh pineapple
100ml full-fat milk
5 scoops coconut ice cream
5 scoops passion fruit sorbet

4 lolly sticks
4 dariole moulds
4 serving glasses

Method

For The Coconut Panna Cotta

Pour the coconut milk and full-fat milk into a saucepan. Split the vanilla pod and scrape the seeds into the milk, along with the sugar. Bring to the boil, remove from heat and leave to infuse for 5 minutes. Squeeze the gelatine to remove any excess water, then add to the warm milk mix. Pour into dariole moulds and leave to set for 3 hours in the fridge.

> **Chef's Tip**
>
> Place a metal tray covered with greaseproof paper in the freezer before making the lollipops. Once the lollipops have been dipped in the white chocolate, leave to set on the frozen tray where they will set quicker and have a better finish.

For The Coconut Lollies

Mould the ice cream into lolly shapes, insert a lolly stick, then place in the freezer to set.

Melt the white chocolate over a *bain-marie*. Dip the lollies in the melted chocolate then sprinkle with desiccated coconut and place in freezer until ready to serve.

For The Piña Colada

Place all the ingredients in a blender and mix until smooth. Place into serving glasses.

To Serve

Serve as pictured

258 WENTBRIDGE HOUSE

The Wentbridge House Hotel, The Great North Road, Wentbridge, Pontefract, West Yorkshire, WF8 3JJ

01977 620 444
www.wentbridgehouse.co.uk Twitter: @wentbridgehouse

Wentbridge House is a beautiful Georgian country house hotel. The building dates back from 1700 and has been open as a hotel since 1960. The hotel is set in 20 acres of grounds in the village of Wentbridge, West Yorkshire.

Steeped in history and surrounded by century old trees, Wentbridge is a hidden gem and offers a luxurious and peaceful retreat from everyday life.

The hotel is independently owned and run with a great deal of care and dedication, ensuring a warm welcome, excellent service and the restful atmosphere that you would expect from a country house hotel.

Wentbridge House has always been passionate about food. Head chef Ian Booth places great emphasis on using fresh, locally sourced produce and the best of British ingredients to produce a wide range of both classic and contemporary dishes.

Experienced and creative chefs offer two dining options, The Fleur de Lys Restaurant and the Wentbridge Brasserie. The Fleur de Lys Restaurant is a true fine dining experience, offering delicious dishes alongside one of the best and most extensive wine lists in Yorkshire which features old favourites and a few surprises. The hugely popular Wentbridge Brasserie is slightly more contemporary and offers an alternative for those wanting tasty comfort food in elegant surroundings. Wentbridge House holds 2 AA Rosettes and has also been awarded Hotel of the Year and Outstanding Customer service with 'Welcome to Yorkshire'.

Open seven days a week for lunch, afternoon tea and dinner.

A warm welcome awaits at Wentbridge House - a perfect venue for private dining and entertaining, whether on a grand or intimate scale. Hotel manager Catherine Harrild and her team focus on delivering delicious food, friendly service and hospitality in a relaxed atmosphere.

GRILLED ASPARAGUS WITH MALTESE DRESSING & CRISPY QUAIL EGGS

SERVES 4

🍷 *A chilled glass of Australian Chardonnay, such as Ad Hoc Hen and Chicken, Cherubino.*

Ingredients

Asparagus

8 white asparagus spears
12 green asparagus spears

Crispy Quail Eggs

12 quail eggs
50g flour
2 egg whites (beaten)
200g panko breadcrumbs
sunflower oil (for frying)

Maltese Dressing

1 banana shallot (chopped)
1 tsp black peppercorns
1 stalk tarragon
1 sprig thyme
150ml white wine vinegar
8 egg yolks
200g butter (melted)
sea salt (to taste)
1 lemon (squeeze of)

Citrus

1 orange or grapefruit
50g sugar
50ml white wine vinegar

Garnish

coriander cress (few sprigs of)

Method

For The Asparagus

Break the asparagus from the tip, trim and peel. *Blanch* the asparagus and grill it to finish just before plating.

For The Crispy Quail Eggs

Cook the eggs in a pan of boiling water for 2 minutes 40 seconds, then lift out into iced water. Peel the eggs, coat in flour, then the egg whites, followed by the breadcrumbs. Fry at the time of service in hot oil until golden brown.

Chef's Tip

The Japanese panko breadcrumb is a rougher, larger flaked breadcrumb which can be found in most supermarkets.

For The Maltese Dressing

Place the shallot, peppercorns, tarragon stalk and thyme in a pan with the vinegar. Reduce by half, then strain through a sieve, saving the liquid.

Make a hollandaise sauce by whisking the yolks in a bowl over a pan of warm water until doubled in volume. Pour the melted butter over the yolks, whisking all the time, taking care to catch the eggs from the sides of the bowl to prevent them from scrambling. Season with salt, add a little of the vinegar reduction and a squeeze of lemon juice, then whisk and taste.

For The Citrus

Peel the orange skin, taking care to remove any pith. Cut into *julienne* and *blanch*. Dissolve the sugar in the white wine vinegar then leave to cool. Add the citrus strips to the pickling liquor.

Remove some of the segments and cut in half. Squeeze the juice and reduce by half. Leave to cool.

To Serve

Place a spoonful of the hollandaise in a clean bowl and add the orange reduction to it. Serve as pictured on an oval plate.

PANACHE OF FISH WITH CITRUS BROTH

SERVES 4

🍷 *A crisp glass of New Zealand Sauvignon Blanc such as 'Saint Clair', Marlborough.*

Ingredients

Panache Of Fish

2 Dover sole (8 fillets, filleted, skinned)
4 king prawns
2 egg whites
75ml double cream
salt (to season)
4 courgette flowers
4 x 50g salmon fillets (skin off)
4 scallops

Citrus Broth

300g mussels
100ml white wine
50ml orange juice
50ml pink grapefruit juice
125ml double cream
salt and pepper (to season)

Pastry

10cm square ready rolled puff pastry
2 egg yolks

Vegetables

8 baby candy beetroot
8 baby carrots
4 baby leeks
8 green asparagus spears

To Serve

1 orange (segmented)
1 pink grapefruit (segmented)
50g pea shoots

Method

For The Panache Of Fish

Carefully wrap 4 of the Dover sole fillets around the king prawns. Blend the remaining 4 fillets with 2 egg whites to a smooth purée, pass through a sieve. Fold in the cream and season with salt.

Pipe the mousse inside the courgette flowers, then wrap in cling film, carefully twisting to make an oval shaped parcel.

> **Chef's Tip**
> Ensure the fish purée and cream are both cold when mixing together otherwise it may split.

For The Citrus Broth

Cook the mussels in the white wine for 2 minutes, remove the mussels and keep separate. Add the orange and grapefruit juices and reduce by half. Add the cream and reduce by half again. Season to taste.

For The Pastry

Preheat the oven to 180°C.

Cut the puff pastry into 4 x 5cm squares. Use the egg yolk to glaze the top of each square and bake for 10 minutes.

For The Vegetables

Prepare and *blanch* the baby vegetables and asparagus.

To Finish And Serve

Carefully poach the salmon, Dover sole and king prawns along with the courgette flowers in seasoned water for 6 minutes.

Sear the scallops in hot oil for 2 minutes on each side.

Serve all the elements of the dish on a warm plate as pictured.

VANILLA PANNA COTTA, TEXTURES OF MANGO

SERVES 4

🍷 *A delicious treat - a glass of French dessert wine, such as Muscat de Beaumes-de-Venise, Domaine de Coyeux, Rhône.*

Ingredients

Panna Cotta

2 whole vanilla pods
275ml double cream
40g caster sugar
2 leaves gelatine (soaked)

Mango Jelly

150ml mango purée
25g caster sugar
50ml water
3 leaves gelatine (soaked)

To Serve

100ml mango purée
1 large ripe mango (peeled)
12 edible viola flowers
12 raspberries
12 blackberries
20g micro lemon balm

4 moulds (tea cup size)

Method

For The Panna Cotta

Carefully split and scrape the vanilla pods. Place into a pan with the double cream and caster sugar. Slowly bring to just below boiling point. Whisk in the soaked gelatine, ensuring that it dissolves.

Place the mixture into the fridge for 5 minutes to cool. Remove the pods, then whisk thoroughly to evenly disperse the vanilla seeds. Divide the mixture evenly between the moulds and set in the fridge for at least 2 hours.

For The Mango Jelly

Add the mango purée to a pan with the caster sugar and water. Place on the heat and bring to a simmer. Whisk the soaked gelatine into the warm mixture until dissolved. Pour into a lined tray and set in the fridge for 2 hours.

To Serve

Create your own unique design on plates of your choice with the mango purée. Slice the ripe mango into thin strips using a peeler and plate as curls. Gently turn out the panna cotta from the moulds, giving the moulds a gentle tap to release. The consistency should have a slight wobble. Decorate as shown.

268
WEST PARK HOTEL

19 West Park, Harrogate, HG1 1BJ

01423 524 471
www.thewestparkhotel.com Twitter: @WestParkHotel

Recently voted Harrogate's Best Newcomer, The West Park Hotel, Restaurant and Bar is the town's destination venue to sleep, eat and drink. This contemporary boutique hotel has been transformed by Provenance Inns & Hotels from the original run-down Victorian coach house into 25 spacious and luxurious bedrooms and suites. The West Park, nestled between designer boutiques, overlooks the beautiful Harrogate Stray, an open area of parkland right in the centre of this historic spa town.

The spacious brasserie restaurant provides all day dining - an extensive breakfast menu for residents and non-residents alike, an à la carte lunch or dinner menu championing hand dived king scallops to a perfect charcoal roasted chateaubriand or a delightfully indulgent dessert, as well as an afternoon tea experience; all showcasing the fantastic local produce at the heart of the menus.

The award-winning, hugely popular cocktail bar features an extensive and innovative cocktail menu, fine wines and Champagnes by the glass, as well as the very best of local ales. This is a sophisticated setting to kick back and relax while good service and attention to detail ensure traditional values.

The terraces are perfect for al fresco dining and drinking, and an exclusive private dining area with its own intimate courtyard is available for business meetings, conferences, events and parties for up to 50 people.

The West Park Hotel combines luxurious design and award-winning décor with exceptional service and hospitality in this city centre destination. Expect a blend of good traditional Yorkshire values with a cosmopolitan twist.

HAND DIVED KING SCALLOPS, CRUSHED SWAYTHORPE PEAS, ROASTED LISHMAN'S BLACK PUDDING, CURED HAM & HERITAGE TOMATOES

SERVES 4

 Picpoul de Pinet 2014, Domaine de Morin Langaran (France)

Ingredients

Scallops

12 hand dived king scallops in shells (roes removed if preferred)
sparkling water (to cover)
15ml olive oil
25g salted butter

Crushed Peas

100ml chicken stock
2 fresh mint leaves
200g sweet garden peas from Swaythorpe Growers, Yorkshire
25g salted butter
salt and pepper (to season)

Black Pudding And Ham

300g Lishman's of Ilkley black pudding
25g salted butter
300g Lishman's of Ilkley air dried York ham (sliced)

Garnish

3 heritage tomatoes
salt and freshly ground black pepper

Method

For The Crushed Peas

Add the chicken stock and mint leaves to a pan, bring to the boil, then add the peas. Cook for 2 minutes, drain and crush using a food blender or potato ricer. Add the butter to the peas and season with salt and pepper.

For The Scallops

Remove the scallops from their shells and place in sparkling water for 10 minutes to remove any sand and debris. Sear the scallops in the olive oil in a hot pan on one side for 2 minutes, then turn and sear for another minute. Add the butter, coat the scallops and remove from the heat to rest.

> **Chef's Tip**
> Coating the scallops in butter enriches the dish by providing shine, a golden brown colour and superior flavour.

For The Black Pudding And Ham

Preheat the oven to 180°C.

Cut the black pudding into 2cm dice. Place onto a baking tray with the butter and roast for 12 minutes.

Place the sliced ham between 2 sheets of parchment paper on a baking tray and bake until crisp, approximately 20 minutes.

For The Garnish

Cut each tomato into quarters and season with salt and pepper.

To Serve

Assemble as pictured.

ROAST DALES LAMB RUMP, SMOKED GARLIC & YORKSHIRE FETTLE MASH, FONDANT CARROT & TURNIP, REDCURRANT & BLACKBERRY JUS

SERVES 4

 Psi 2010, Peter Sisseck, Ribera Del Duero
(Spain)

Ingredients

Roast Lamb Rump

4 x 170g Yorkshire Dales lamb rump
1 tbsp vegetable oil
salt and pepper

Garlic And Yorkshire Fettle Mash

800ml duck fat
1 whole bulb smoked garlic
500g red potatoes (peeled, diced into 5cm cubes)
100g cold butter (cubed)
200ml double cream (reduced to 100ml)
100g Shepherd's Purse Yorkshire Fettle cheese
1 tsp ground white pepper

Fondant Carrot And Turnip

200g Chantenay carrots
200g baby turnips
80g salted butter
1 tbsp chopped chives

Redcurrant And Blackberry Jus

1 litre veal stock (reduced to 200ml)
1 sprig fresh redcurrants
8 fresh blackberries

Method

For The Garlic And Yorkshire Fettle Mash

Preheat the oven to 130°C.

Heat the duck fat, submerge the whole bulb of garlic in the fat and *confit* for 3 hours. Remove the garlic and leave to cool. Squeeze the cloves into a small bowl and whisk with a fork. Add the diced potatoes to a pan of cold water and bring to the boil, then reduce the heat and simmer for 25 minutes. Mash with a potato ricer, add the cold butter, reduced double cream, Fettle cheese and white pepper, mixing until smooth. Add the smoked garlic and incorporate into the mash.

> **Chef's Tip**
>
> To *confit* the garlic in duck fat provides an exceptionally soft texture, perfect to create a very smooth mash potato.

For The Roast Lamb Rump

Preheat the oven to 180°C.

Season the lamb rumps with salt and pepper, seal in a hot pan with the vegetable oil, skin side down first until golden on each side. Roast, skin side down, for 12 minutes in the same pan.

For The Fondant Carrot And Turnip

Cook the Chantenay carrots and baby turnips in boiling water until tender. Heat the butter in a shallow saucepan and fry the carrots and turnips until golden brown. Remove from the heat, and add the chopped chives.

For The Redcurrant And Blackberry Jus

Bring the veal stock to the boil, add the blackberries and redcurrants, simmer for 1-2 minutes until the berries soften.

To Serve

Carve each lamb rump into 3 slices. Serve on top of the smoked garlic mash with the golden baby vegetables at the side. Finish with the berries and jus.

LEMON CURD, PISTACHIO SPONGE

SERVES 8

 Château Briatte 2009, Sauternes (France)

Ingredients

Lemon Curd

125ml lemon juice
1 lemon (zest of)
90g egg yolks (from 4-5 eggs)
45g eggs (about 1 medium egg)
125g caster sugar
125g unsalted butter (cut into cubes, chilled)

For The Pistachio Sponge

175g unsalted butter (softened)
175g caster sugar
3 free range eggs
175g self-raising flour
5g baking powder
2 tsp pistachio purée

For The Garnish

raspberry sorbet
20 fresh raspberries
2 tbsp freeze dried raspberries
20 mini meringues
2 tbsp pistachios (finely chopped)
8 dehydrated lemon slices
micro herbs

2 x 20cm round baking tins
(or a 27cm x 18cm rectangular tin)

Method

For The Lemon Curd

Reduce the lemon juice with the zest in a pan over a low heat to two thirds of the original volume. Whisk the yolks and whole egg together until combined, add the sugar and whisk until dissolved. Add the warm lemon juice to the yolk mix. Thicken the mix over a pan of simmering water, stirring continuously for approximately 20 minutes. Whisk in the butter, 2 or 3 cubes at a time. When all the butter is incorporated, strain the lemon curd through a fine sieve or *chinois* while warm. Leave to cool and set before use.

For The Pistachio Sponge

Preheat the oven to 180°C.

Cream the softened butter and sugar together until pale and fluffy. Add the eggs, one at a time and whisk into the mixture. Combine the flour and baking powder, then fold into the sponge mix a little at a time. Add the pistachio purée and mix in well. Pour into a lined tray or cake tins. Bake for 15-20 minutes.

Chef's Tip

Buy pistachio purée instead of blending your own pistachios - the colour and flavour from this great product is fantastic.

To Serve

Spread a tablespoon of the lemon curd across a shallow plate and add one scoop of the raspberry sorbet on top. Cut the cooled pistachio sponge into triangles and arrange on the plate with the berries, nuts and meringue. Garnish with dehydrated lemon slices and micro herbs.

278
THE WESTWOOD RESTAURANT

New Walk, Beverley, East Yorkshire, HU17 7AE

01482 881 999
www.thewestwood.co.uk Twitter: @The_Westwood

Twins Matthew and Michele Barker are the partnership and passion behind the Westwood Restaurant. Since opening in 2007 their focus has been on serving up high quality, locally sourced ingredients, showcasing the best the region has to offer.

The Westwood has become one of the most popular restaurants in East Yorkshire. Situated in the historic market town of Beverley, between York and Hull, The Westwood is just a short walk from the Westwood Pasture offering stunning views of the black mill, the race course and Beverley Minster. Set in the grounds of Beverley's former Grade II listed Georgian courthouse, The Westwood's contemporary interior blends beautifully with the period features and charm of this historic building.

For Matthew, cooking is about getting the best out of the ingredients and delivering beautiful plates packed with great flavour. The Westwood believes in making the most of the seasons so the menu is constantly changing to bring you the best of locally sourced produce - beef sourced from North Yorkshire and seafood caught off Yorkshire's East coast feature heavily.

Enjoy a relaxing meal in modern, elegant surroundings. Dine outdoors on the spacious garden terrace. Experience the action of a professional kitchen at the chef's table. Whether you're joining them for a light lunch, an evening meal or a special occasion, you can always look forward to a warm welcome, a relaxed atmosphere and friendly service.

THE WESTWOOD
RESTAURANT

01482 881999

Experience the heart of The Westwood's service first hand at the chef's table. Absorb the atmosphere and the action of a professional kitchen whilst you enjoy your meal with a 'behind the scenes' view.

ENGLISH ASPARAGUS, SAUCE GRIBICHE, CRISP HEN EGG, SUMMER TRUFFLE

SERVES 4

 Picpoul de Pinet La Côte Flamenc, Languedoc-Roussillon, 2014 (France)

Ingredients

Crisp Hen Eggs

4 eggs
vinegar (splash of)
100g plain flour (seasoned)
1 egg (beaten)
150g panko breadcrumb

Sauce Gribiche

4 eggs
1 tbsp Dijon mustard
1 tbsp Champagne vinegar
4 tbsp grapeseed oil
1 tbsp crème fraîche
1 tbsp parsley (chopped)
1 tbsp chives (chopped)
1 tbsp gherkins (chopped)
1 tbsp fine capers (chopped)
salt and ground white pepper (to season)

Asparagus

2 bunches English asparagus (peeled)
butter (knob of)
salt and pepper (to season)

To Finish

summer truffle (grated)
rapeseed oil (drizzle of)
mustard frill

Method

For The Crisp Hen Eggs

Poach the eggs for 3 minutes in a deep pan of simmering water with a good splash of vinegar, then place in ice cold water. When cooled completely, transfer to a tray. Using 3 bowls, roll the eggs carefully first in flour, then coat in beaten egg and finish with panko breadcrumbs. Set aside.

For The Sauce Gribiche

Boil the eggs in salted water for 6 minutes, then cool in ice cold water. Peel the eggs, then separate the yolks from the whites. Finely chop the egg whites and set aside. Place the yolks in a food processor or blender with the mustard and vinegar and blend. Slowly pour the oil, in a fine stream, to create a mayonnaise. Fold in the chopped egg white and remaining ingredients. Season with salt and pepper.

For The Asparagus

Submerge the asparagus in boiling, salted water for about 5 minutes until tender. Drain, season with melted butter and salt and pepper.

Chef's Tip

Only serve this dish when English asparagus is in season, usually for 8 weeks from April to June.

To Serve

Place the asparagus in the centre of the plate. Serve a good tablespoon of the sauce gribiche on top. Just prior to serving, deep fry the crisp hen eggs (180°C) until golden for a maximum of 2 minutes to ensure the egg yolk is runny inside. Season with salt and finish with grated summer truffle and rapeseed oil.

'WESTWOOD' BONE-IN RIBEYE STEAK MARINATED IN MOLASSES, BOURBON & THYME WITH CAFE DE PARIS GRILL BUTTER

SERVES 2-4

Cabernet Sauvignon, Black Stallion Winery,
2012, Napa Valley (USA)

Ingredients

1kg aged bone-in rib
(or 4 x 227g aged ribeye or fillet steaks)
olive oil

Molasses Marinade

thyme (few sprigs of)
1 red chilli (halved, deseeded)
3 cloves garlic (finely chopped)
1 thumb fresh ginger (grated)
50ml bourbon
50ml water
25ml balsamic vinegar
1 tbsp cracked black pepper
350g molasses syrup
1 tsp dried chilli flakes

Café de Paris Grill Butter

1 red onion (chopped)
1 clove garlic (chopped)
salt and pepper (to taste)
250g butter (softened)
10g each of thyme, parsley and tarragon (chopped)
1½ tsp Dijon mustard
1½ tsp Gentleman's relish
1 tbsp Worcestershire sauce
1½ tsp brown sauce
30ml port or sherry
½ lemon (juice of)

Method

For The Molasses Marinade

Gently cook the thyme, red chilli, garlic and ginger in a little oil in a deep pan for 5 minutes. Add the rest of the ingredients and bring to the boil, then simmer for 10 minutes. Set aside and leave to cool completely. Brush the raw steaks with the molasses marinade and leave for a minimum of 2-3 hours.

> **Chef's Tip**
>
> For best results, make the marinade the day before. A 1kg aged bone-in rib can be prepared by a good high street butcher, however the marinade works equally well with 227g rib eye or fillet steak.

For The Café de Paris Grill Butter

Heat the onions, garlic, salt and pepper in a pan with 20g of butter and cook gently for 4-5 minutes. Transfer to a bowl, then add all the other ingredients to make the butter, shape into cylinders in cling film or parchment paper and refrigerate until needed.

For The Steak

Preheat the oven to 180°C or 200°C (fan).

Rub a griddle pan with olive oil and heat on the stove until very hot.

For 200g steaks (180°C fan): Season the meat well and sear on both sides for 2 minutes, then transfer to the oven for 2-3 minutes for medium rare. Extend or reduce cooking time as you prefer.

For 1kg rib (200°C fan): Place in the oven for 20 minutes for medium rare. Because of the high sugar content in the marinade, the beef will blacken - don't worry as this adds to the flavour of the beef.

To Serve

Serve the steak with melted Café de Paris butter.

BUTTERSCOTCH POT DE CREME, SALTED CARAMEL, COCONUT CREAM, COCONUT WAFER

SERVES 8

 Planeta Passito di Noto, 2012 (Sicily)

Ingredients

Coconut Cream

100g desiccated coconut
568ml double cream
1 tbsp icing sugar

Butterscotch Cream

50g soft dark brown sugar
water (a few tablespoons of)
1.7 litres double cream
1 vanilla pod (split)
½ tsp salt
12 egg yolks
50g caster sugar

Salted Caramel Sauce (Makes 250ml)

200g caster sugar
200ml double cream
¼ tsp fleur de sel or coarse sea salt (to taste)
20g unsalted butter

Coconut Wafer

50g unsalted butter
45g liquid glucose
90g caster sugar
35g plain flour
15g desiccated coconut

To Serve

toasted coconut
lemon biscotti

8 glass ramekins

Method

For The Coconut Cream (Prepare ahead)

Combine the desiccated coconut and double cream and leave to *macerate* overnight, or up to 2 days for best results. When you're ready to serve the cream, pass the coconut mixture through a sieve, then add the icing sugar to sweeten the cream. Gently whisk the cream until it just starts to thicken, being careful not to over whip. Place into a piping bag.

For The Butterscotch Cream (Prepare ahead)

Using a deep, heavy bottomed pan, mix the soft brown sugar and water until it feels like wet sand. Stir over a high heat until it caramelises, then add the double cream, salt and vanilla pod Cook on a gentle simmer until the sugar has dissolved.

Whisk the egg yolks and caster sugar in a bowl until pale. Slowly add this to the butterscotch cream. Turn the heat right down, then gently thicken the custard mixture until it coats the back of a spoon. Pour into glass ramekins and leave to set in the fridge for minimum of 5 hours, or for best results overnight.

For The Salted Caramel Sauce

Add the caster sugar to a heavy bottomed pan and cook on a medium heat until it starts to caramelise and turns a deep golden brown. Using a wooden spoon, stir the sugar until all the sugar crystals have dissolved, then add the cream very slowly as this will boil up quite quickly. Simmer until combined, add the fleur de sel and the butter, then pass through a fine sieve. Set aside.

For The Coconut Wafer

Preheat the oven to 180°C (fan).

Melt the butter and liquid glucose over a *bain-marie*, then stir in the caster sugar, flour and desiccated coconut until well incorporated. Allow the mixture to cool in the fridge.

Line a baking tray with a non-stick baking sheet. Roll the cooled mixture into small balls, then press the balls onto the sheet about 7cm apart. Bake for 4-6 minutes. Leave to cool completely.

To Assemble The Dish

Pour a little salted caramel sauce on top of the set butterscotch cream. Pipe the coconut cream on top. Finish with toasted coconut and coconut wafer as pictured.

> **Chef's Tip**
>
> Start the preparation for this dessert the day before as the coconut cream needs a minimum of 24 hours to stand in your fridge to achieve maximum flavour.

288
WYNYARD
HALL HOTEL

The Wellington Restaurant at The Wynyard Hall Hotel, Tees Valley, TS22 5NF

01740 644 811
www.wynyardhall.co.uk Twitter: @WynyardHall

Set within 150 acres of historical landscaped parkland, this impressive 4 star hotel, on the fringes of Durham in the Tees Valley, offers a winning combination of elegant grandeur and contemporary comfort.

From its stunning function rooms, which can cater for 15 to 240 guests for birthday or christening parties, wedding receptions or corporate events, to its 19 individually designed bedrooms and suites plus three cottages, it is the perfect venue for any occasion.

Its renowned multi AA Rosette restaurant, The Wellington, offers an ever changing menu of modern British dishes created with the finest local ingredients, while those looking to unwind can enjoy a range of beauty and body treatments in the tranquil surroundings of the lakeside spa.

The Wellington Restaurant sets the precedence for all aspects of the large multi-outlet operation. From this formidable level of service offered, comes a demand for a superior calibre of chef, not only to produce, but to continuously maintain their ever progressing standards.

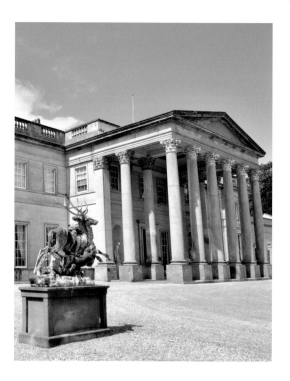

The employees are committed professionals who dedicate their time and innovative skills to ensuring fantastic customer service in a world class setting.

Discipline, respect, resilience.

GOOSE LIVER GANACHE, BLOOD ORANGE & GINGERBREAD

SERVES 4

 Palmina Alisos 2004 Pinot Grigio
(USA)

Ingredients

Goose Liver Ganache

500g goose liver
4 juniper berries (bashed)
1.9g sel rose
2g table salt
30ml double cream

Blood Orange Jelly

200ml blood orange purée
3 sheets gelatine (softened)

Gingerbread

150g light rye flour
100g plain white flour
80g medium oatmeal
90g dark muscovado sugar
20g baking powder
½ tsp ground cinnamon
½ tsp ground cardamom
½ tsp ground caraway seed
2 tsp ground ginger
½ tsp ground nutmeg
1 tsp grated lemon zest
1 tsp grated orange zest
280ml clear runny honey
120ml milk
8 eggs (medium)

Cherry Gel

100g fresh cherries
50ml cherry purée
30g ultratex

Garnish

lemon balm leaves
pea shoots
edible flowers

medium size loaf tin (lined)

Method

For The Goose Liver Ganache

Vacuum seal the goose liver and juniper. Place in a thermo circulator for 1½ hours at 65°C. Alternatively, gently poach in a sealed bag.

After cooking, blend with the sel rose, table salt and double cream until *emulsified*. Pass through a fine sieve twice and pour into a desired mould or plate. Leave to set in the fridge for 2 hours.

> **Chef's Tip**
>
> Ensure the goose liver is at room temperature before beginning the cooking process to facilitate a consistent core temperature.

For The Blood Orange Jelly

Gently warm the blood orange purée and stir in the gelatine. Pass through a sieve and set over the cooked goose liver ganache.

For The Gingerbread

Preheat the oven to 170°C (fan).

Sieve all the dry ingredients.

Mix all the ingredients together, place into the prepared loaf tin and bake for 25 minutes. Cool, then freeze. Slice on a meat slicer and dehydrate for 1 hour at 45°C.

For The Cherry Gel

Blend the fresh cherries, cherry purée and ultratex. Pass through a fine sieve and refrigerate for 2 hours minimum.

To Serve

Dot the cherry gel on top of the orange jelly and garnish with the gingerbread, flowers, pea shoots and lemon balm leaves.

ORGANIC CHICKEN, SMOKED SWEET POTATO & LOBSTER CROQUETTE, SUMMER TRUFFLE

SERVES 4

Cloudy Bay, Sauvignon Blanc, Marlborough 2013 (New Zealand)

Ingredients

1 lobster

Lobster Sauce

2kg lobster shells
1 carrot (diced)
1 stick celery (diced)
1 onion (diced)
water (to cover)
5g agar agar

Smoked Sweet Potato And Lobster Croquette

1 large sweet potato (diced)
oak chips (to smoke)
100ml double cream
50ml water
2 x lobster claws (from the whole lobster, poached)
80g tarragon (finely chopped)
100g parsley (finely chopped)
flour, beaten egg, panko breadcrumbs (to *pane*)

Chicken Roulade

2 organic chicken supremes (boneless)
50g black truffle (blended)
20ml truffle oil

Vegetables

10 asparagus spears
4 baby nave
100g garden peas
100g broad beans
5g nutmeg, 5g mace
50g butter

Garnish

pea shoots
horseradish shoots

4 x 12cm ring moulds

Method

For The Lobster Sauce (Allow 48 hours)

Sauté the *mirepoix* until tender, add the lobster shells and cover with water. Simmer for 1 hour. Ice filtrate - leave to cool, then freeze in a suitable container. Once frozen, remove from the container and set in a colander lined with 2 sheets of muslin over a bowl. Keep in the fridge and allow to melt slowly, for 24 - 36 hours. Any impurities will be caught in the muslin and you will be left with a clear consommé. Add the agar agar to half the consomme and set in the ring moulds. Reserve the remainder.

For The Smoked Sweet Potato And Lobster Croquette

Smoke the sweet potato, then gently simmer in the cream and water until tender. Combine with the claw meat and tarragon and season to taste. Roll into long roulades with cling film and freeze. Mix the parsley into the panko breadcrumbs. Once firm, remove the film and *pane*. Bake in the oven for 8 minutes at 170°C (fan) when you're ready to serve.

For The Chicken Roulade

Make a paste with the blended fresh truffles and truffle oil. Gently lift the chicken skin, fill with the paste and roll tightly in cling film to form a roulade. Slow steam the chicken at 60°C for 1 hour. Alternatively, gently poach at 60°C.

For The Vegetables

Trim the asparagus and cook with the broad beans and peas in a butter, mace and nutmeg *emulsion*. Poach the nave in a butter and water *emulsion*.

For The Lobster Tail

Cook the lobster tail in salted, boiling water for 7½ minutes, then place into an ice bath. Portion and reheat in butter to serve.

> **Chef's Tip**
> Tie the lobster straight before cooking to ensure accurate portion control.

To Serve

Position the set lobster sauce on the plates, halve the chicken roulades, then place all the elements on top as pictured. Gently heat the remaining lobster sauce and pour over at the table.

ICED WOODLAND BERRY

SERVES 4

 Egon Müller Wiltinger Braune Kupp Riesling
Spätlese 2010 (Germany)

Ingredients

Parfait

100g caster sugar
75g egg yolk (about 4 yolks)
175g cherry purée
200ml double cream (semi-whipped)
100g cloudberries
100g bilberries
100g freeze dried blackberries

Blackberry Gel

100g blackberry purée
20g sugar
1g agar agar
stock syrup (to blend)

To Serve

dehydrated candied lemon

parfait moulds (of your choice)

Method

For The Parfait (Prepare the day before)

Boil the sugar to 121°C. Whisk into the egg yolks until white and fluffy (*sabayon*). Keep whisking until cold, then fold in the cherry purée. Fold the berries into the semi-whipped cream mixture and carefully fold into the *sabayon*. Fill the moulds and freeze overnight.

Decant from the moulds and roll in freeze dried blackberries.

> **Chef's Tip**
>
> Ensure the parfait mixture is rested at a temperature below -18°C for a minimum of 24 hours.

For The Blackberry Gel

Boil the purée with the sugar and agar agar for approximately 2 minutes. Remove from the heat and place into a container. Allow to set, then blend and add stock syrup until the desired consistency is reached.

For The Candied Lemon

Dehydrate the candied lemon in a dehydrator or low oven (45°C) for 24 hours.

To Serve

Pipe the blackberry gel onto the plate and top with the lightly crushed candied lemon. Sit the parfait on top and serve immediately.

298
YOREBRIDGE HOUSE

Bainbridge, Leyburn, North Yorkshire, DL8 3EE

01969 652 060
www.yorebridgehouse.co.uk Twitter: @YorebridgeHouse

Yorebridge House, in the Yorkshire Dales, is a luxury boutique hotel and restaurant situated by the river on the edge of the unspoilt village of Bainbridge, Wensleydale, surrounded by beautiful countryside.

With stunning backdrops of rolling hills and rivers, the Victorian Grade II listed former Headmaster's House and School sits proud and welcoming, promising luxury, relaxation and beautiful interiors with superb 3 AA Rosette menus, bespoke AA awarded notable wine list and a personal, professional service from the moment you arrive.

David and Charlotte Reilly lovingly restored the property in 2006, transforming it into a contemporary but cosy oasis of calm, bringing a unique design to each and every element of the hotel. Driven by their joy in sharing their passion for luxury, fine dining, quality, comfort and the good old Yorkshire Dales with their guests, they work hard to keep everything truly 'Yorkshire' and invest time to ensure every element of their offering is as perfect as it can be.

The unique bedrooms, inspired by their travels, boast fabulous views, luxury products and some rooms even allow you to soak away in your own private outdoor hot tub.

The restaurant is calm and peaceful as light streams in through the French windows with views over the Yorkshire Dales, but by night, is dark and candle-lit, where guests can linger in an atmosphere of decadence.

Multi award-winning Yorebridge House has held 3 AA Rosettes since 2014 rewarding the team for their inspiring, innovative dishes using superb local produce. Dishes excel in design and flavour and the restaurant is famous for its romantic atmosphere.

YORKSHIRE QUAIL & BBQ SWEETCORN

SERVES 4

🍷 *2010 Prima, DO Toro, Bodegas Maurodos (Spain)*
A low alcohol, deep flavoured Spanish red will
complement the chorizo element of the dish.
Something like a Tempranillo, usually oak aged,
this would also enhance the spices of the dish.

Method

For The Yorkshire Quail

Preheat the oven to 95°C (fan).

Submerge the quail legs in the duck fat and bake for 1 hour or until tender.

Preheat the oven to 185°C (fan).

Stuff the cavity of each breast with a sprig of thyme and clove of garlic. Cook the breasts on the crown for 10 minutes in the oven. After slow cooking the legs, place them back in the oven with the breasts to crisp up.

Leave to rest for 10 minutes, then remove the breasts from the crown.

> **Chef's Tip**
> You can buy the quail ready prepared from your local quality butcher.

To Serve

Place the used garlic and thyme in a hot pan with the wine and cooking juices. Reduce to a sauce consistency and finish with butter. Scorch the sweetcorn with a blow torch to give it a BBQ flavour. Pan fry the chorizo and serve as pictured. Garnish with popcorn shoots.

Ingredients

Yorkshire Quail

4 Yorkshire quails (remove legs and *French trim*)
200ml duck fat (or enough to cover legs)
4 sprigs thyme
4 cloves garlic
300ml white wine (Chardonnay works well)
20g butter

To Serve

sweetcorn (steamed)
Yorkshire chorizo (pan fried)
popcorn shoots

(see glossary)

BELLY PORK WITH PAN FRIED SQUID & CARROTS

SERVES 4

🍷 *2012 Riesling Muenchberg, Grand Cru, Domaine André Ostertag (France)*

Ingredients

Belly Pork

500g trim belly pork (skin on)
1 onion (sliced)
2 carrots (chopped)
1 garlic clove
1 star anise
1 sprig thyme
1 stick lemongrass
butter (knob of)
honey (drizzle of)

Squid

1 squid
olive oil (drizzle of)

Carrot Purée

400g carrots
25g butter
salt (to taste)

Pickled Carrots

2 bunches baby carrots (cleaned)
50ml white wine vinegar
50ml water
50g caster sugar
1 star anise
chilli flakes (pinch of)
1 sprig coriander

Sauce

100ml good quality chicken stock
10ml sherry vinegar
25ml runny honey
200ml veal stock

Garnish

coriander leaves

Method

For The Belly Pork

Preheat the oven to 170°C (fan).

Place the pork in an oven tray with the vegetables and aromats and cover with water. Cover the tray with tin foil and cook in the oven for 2 hours.

When cooked, remove the pork from the tray and place it in the fridge to cool.

Once cool, cut into portions.

For The Squid

Slice the raw squid into 2cm thick rings. Sear in a hot pan with a small amount of olive oil for 1½ minutes or until golden brown.

For The Carrot Purée

Boil the carrots until soft. Drain, then blend with the butter until smooth, adding salt to taste.

For The Pickled Carrots

Bring all the ingredients, except the carrots, to the boil. Add the carrots and boil for 1 minute. Remove from the heat and leave to cool in the pickling liquor.

For The Sauce

Bring all the ingredients to the boil.

To Serve

Preheat the oven to 180°C (fan).

To re-heat the pork, cook in the oven for 5 minutes, or until the skin is crispy. Finish with butter and honey. Assemble all other elements of the dish as pictured. Garnish with coriander.

> **Chef's Tip**
> Buy the squid ready prepped from your local fishmonger. Good chicken stock can be purchased in most delis.

CHOCOLATE DOME

SERVES 8

William Pickering, Tawny Port (Portugal)
The best pairing with milk chocolate, tawny port!
Subtle and silky, there should be some nutty, spicy
and fruity notes to balance the sweetness of the
dessert. Choose one that is reasonably young, 20
years maximum.

Ingredients

Chocolate Brownie

170g milk chocolate
170g butter
250g caster sugar
140g self-raising flour
3 medium eggs

Chocolate Cream

200g caster sugar
75g egg yolk (about 4 yolks)
250g milk chocolate
200ml full-fat milk
320ml double cream
2 leaves gelatine (soaked)

Chocolate Glaze

300g dark chocolate
30g cocoa butter

To Serve

praline ice cream
chocolate soil

20cm x 30cm baking tin
8 dariole moulds

Method

For The Chocolate Brownie

Preheat the oven to 140°C (fan).

Melt the chocolate and butter until smooth. Add the sugar, flour and eggs and stir until blended together and smooth. Pour into the baking tray and bake for 30 minutes or until firm to touch on top. Once cool, use the dariole moulds to cut out the brownie shape and place to one side.

For The Chocolate Cream

Whisk the sugar and egg yolks together until light and fluffy. Melt the chocolate with the milk and cream, then stir in the gelatine until blended. Combine both mixtures together until smooth, then pour into the bottom of the dariole moulds. Place the brownie cut outs on top of the chocolate cream mixture. Transfer to the freezer to set for 12 hours, or ideally overnight.

For The Chocolate Glaze

Mix both ingredients in a bowl over hot water until melted and smooth.

To Serve

Take the chocolate cream and brownie out of the freezer. Remove from the moulds and pour over the glaze. Garnish with a scoop of praline ice cream and chocolate soil.

> **Chef's Tip**
> Prepare all elements of this dish, except the glaze, in advance.

308
LOCAL FOOD AMBASSADORS

For the past 25 years, three chefs have constantly reinvested in the North East and Yorkshire food scene to create some of the area's best loved restaurants. Each are advocates of sourcing the best local ingredients and use their culinary expertise to develop and inspire the next generation of home grown talent.

Terry Laybourne

Born in Newcastle, Terry Laybourne has been at the top of his game from the moment he opened 21 Queen Street in the city in 1988.

Having brought the first Michelin star to the North East in 1992 and being awarded the MBE in 1998, Terry has inspired a generation of chefs while helping change perceptions of the region's culinary scene.

Terry Laybourne

He now presides over the 21 Hospitality Group - a collection of some of the North East's most highly regarded restaurants including the recently rebranded 21, Caffé Vivo, Café 21 at Fenwick, Ko Sai, The Saltwater Fish Co and The Broad Chare.

He has also been involved in other restaurant-based ventures including the creation of the Newcastle 4 star, boutique hotel Jesmond Dene House - picking up numerous awards along the way.

A major road accident while an apprentice chef kept Terry off work for 18 months during a critical time in his career. So, unable to cook he committed his time to reading and absorbing cookery theory, laying the foundations for his stellar rise on recovery.

He spent time in the Channel Islands, Germany and Switzerland before settling back in his beloved North East.

Terry is a huge advocate of local producers featuring many locally sourced ingredients in his menus. His team are like his family, with many starting their careers as apprentices and moving on to senior roles within the group.

James MacKenzie

James Mackenzie started work in kitchens aged 13 washing up while growing up on the North Yorkshire coast in Filey.

He trained at Scarborough Technical College before learning his trade in top kitchens across the UK. James came back to Yorkshire as head chef at The Star Inn in Harome, in 1992.

It was in March 2006 that James and his wife Kate took on the Pipe and Glass Inn in South Dalton, Beverley in East Yorkshire and transformed it through a major refurbishment.

The bar has kept a country pub feel, while the restaurant is warm, welcoming and airy, with a conservatory which looks out over the garden and has a spectacular long table for up to 28 people. Upstairs, the Hotham Room is available for private dining for up to ten people, and has its own separate lounge and demonstration kitchen.

He also set up MGB Consultants providing first class dining for GNER trains.

Marcus took over The Bay Horse at Hurworth, near Darlington, in late 2008 with his old friend and business partner, Jonathan Hall. The pair have turned the pub's fortunes around by investing in a stunning re-fit and offering outstanding food, ale and customer service.

They have since jointly opened two more restaurants - Muse, a continental café and Cena, an Italian, both in Yarm.

As well as being named Gastropub Chef of the Year, Marcus has played a key role in The Bay Horse winning a string of accolades including the Michelin Bib Gourmand for six consecutive years. It has also been named in the Top 50 Best Pubs in the UK, according to the Good Food Guide, for the last two years, has featured as an Inspectors' Favourite in the Michelin Eating Out in Pubs Guide and the Top 10 Gastropubs in the UK.

Marcus also has a regular food column in the Middlesbrough Gazette and a fortnightly slot on BBC Tees radio.

James MacKenzie

The Pipe and Glass became East Yorkshire's first and only Michelin Star restaurant in 2010 - an accolade it has retained - as well as winning a clutch of awards whether it be for the pub or the restaurant.

James is passionate about providing great East Yorkshire hospitality, using where possible the best locally-sourced ingredients, whether the customer is dropping in for a steak sandwich and a pint or a special celebration meal.

He has appeared on TV, has his own book, runs cookery classes and is a true inspiration to would-be chefs.

Marcus Bennett

Marcus Bennett has been a chef for over 25 years and his expertise has won him a string of awards and recognition amongst his peers.

He jointly owns three very different restaurants in the North East, but each with one common theme, exceptional food in fantastic surroundings.

He was head chef at The Tontine and set up McCoys at The Baltic and in Yarm. Marcus worked abroad for a few years, most notably at a restaurant in the Caribbean where he cooked for Princess Diana, and at a leading hotel in Quebec, Canada where he worked in a French kitchen.

Marcus Bennett

FISH

CARRICKS OF SNAPE
Yew Tree House, Snape, North Yorkshire, DL8 2TJ.
T: 01677 470 261 www.carrickfishltd.co.uk
Supplier of fish and shellfish, as well as local fruit and vegetables.

HODGSON FISH
5 Whitby Street, Hartlepool, TS24 7AD.
T: 01429 273 169 www.hodgsonfish.co.uk
Delivers fresh, high quality fish and shellfish daily.

LINDISFARNE SEAFOODS LTD
2 Cliffords Fort, North Shields, Tyne and Wear, NE30 1JE.
T: 0191 259 2909 www.fish-quay.com
Suppliers of the finest variety of crabs, langoustines, lobsters and shellfish on the North Shields Fish Quay.

FRANK ROUND LTD
5 Prospect Terrace, North Shields, Tyne and Wear, NE30 1DX.
T: 0191 257 1632
Supplies the finest day boat fish, direct to your door daily.

WHITBY CATCH
1 Pier Road, Whitby, North Yorkshire, YO21 3PT.
T: 01947 601 313 www.thewhitbycatch.co.uk
Traditional fishmongers and online fish and shellfish merchant.

WINES/BEERS

BERKMANN WINE CELLAR
16 Marston Moor Business Park, Rudgate, Tockwith, North Yorkshire, YO26 7QF.
T: 01423 357 567 www.berkmann.co.uk

DURHAM BREWERY
Bowburn North Industrial Estate, Bowburn, Durham, County Durham, DH6 5PF.
T: 0191 377 1991 www.durhambrewery.co.uk
Selection of artisan beers.

NEWHOUSES WINE MERCHANTS LEVENSDALE HOUSE
Ayton Road, Stokesley, North Yorkshire, TS9 5JW.
T: 01642 714 046 www.newhouseswine.co.uk
Offering a range of wines from across the globe.

MEAT

FREEMAN BUTCHERS
353A Dukesway Court, Team Valley Trading Estate,
Gateshead, Tyne and Wear, NE11 0BH.
T: 0191 456 0297 www.freemancateringbutchers.co.uk

J D Halls
2 Hill Street, Corbridge, NE45 5AA.
T: 01434 632 005
*Top drawer butcher supplying delicious cuts and very, very
tasty black pudding.*

THE GARDEN AT WYNYARD HALL CAFE & FARM SHOP
Wynyard Hall Hotel, Tees Valley, TS22 5NF
01740 644 811 www.wynyardhall.co.uk Twitter: @WynyardHall

The Gardens project is the dream and vision of Sir John Hall. It was designed and
created by multi RHS award-winning landscape architect Alistair Baldwin along with
rose expert Michael Marriott, from David Austin Roses.

From floribundas and climbing roses to the
classic English rose, The Gardens are home
to over 3,000 roses and, when finished, are
set to be one of the largest rose gardens in
the UK. An array of carefully chosen flowers,
shrubs and trees sit alongside beautiful
water features.

Visitors can relax with drinks, cakes, pastries
or a signature hot dish of the day in the café
overlooking the beautiful flowers.

Guests may also browse the farm shop
which showcases the finest artisan produce
the North East has to offer including freshly
baked bread, artisan cheese, lovely gifts, the
best local sausages and homemade pasta
sauces and relishes.

HAPPY ORGANIC
Front Street, Cleadon Village, Sunderland, SR6 7PG
T: 0191 536 3623 www.happyorganic.org Twitter: @happyorganicNE

Happy Organic features a café and specialist store selling local, organic and natural products. They have a great range of gluten-free, dairy-free and wheat-free products with all vegetables, eggs, fish and fruit sourced locally. There is also an impressive range of wines and spirits, whole foods, organic flours, home-baked breads from Food For Thought bakers, meat from Eversfield Organic & Duchy Organic farms, organic free range eggs from Harry Hodgson in County Durham, organic smoked salmon by Inverawe Smokehouses in Scotland, organic milk from Acorn Dairy in Darlington, health supplements and now eco-friendly washing products. Company owner and BANT qualified nutritionist, Luisa Mordain says "Healthy eating has always been close to my heart. With my family involvement in a number of North East food companies, you could say food is in my blood. I used to love visiting places like this down south and I wanted to create a little bit of what I saw and experienced, here in the North East."

In the café you can expect sweet treats, including homemade banana loaf, raw brownies, scones and 'posh jammy dodgers' to go with your Italian fair-trade organic coffee or heartier offerings such as Tuscan bean soup, quiche, frittata and one pot wonders. Organic tapas nights are a regular feature on Friday evenings.

It's a family affair
Dad, Romano Minchella, co-owns Bistro Romano, directly opposite Happy Organic on Front Street with his brother Paolo. Here you will find everything from freshly prepared pasta dishes to steak medallions with a brandy cream sauce, all accompanied with an extensive wine list.

FARMISON & CO

Charter Road, Canal Side, Ripon HG4, 1AJ.
T: 01765 601 226 www.farmison.com
*Farmison & Co supply are a specialist butcher and game
dealer, supplying the very best Yorkshire has to offer;
named breeds from individually named farms.*

LISHMAN'S OF ILKLEY AWARD-WINNING YORKSHIRE BUTCHERS

25 Leeds Road, Ilkley, West Yorkshire, LS29 8DP.
T: 01943 609 436 www.lishmansonline.co.uk

*Lishman's of Ilkley is a multi award-winning
butcher in the spa town of Ilkley, nestled at the
gateway to the Yorkshire Dales. Sourcing the
majority of meat from established Yorkshire farms,
Lishman's supports regional farmers who share
their commitment to welfare and outstanding
quality. Provenance is paramount at Lishman's;
almost everything in the shop is prepared entirely
in-house with particular renown for exceptional
sausages, bacon, hams and homemade pies.*

R&J YORKSHIRE'S FINEST FARMERS & BUTCHERS

Water Edge, Longswales Lane, Ripon, HG4 3RR.
T: 01765 658 611 www.randjyorkshiresfinest.co.uk
Well aged and matured meat delivered daily from a family run business (est 1978) supplying high quality meat to catering establishments throughout Yorkshire. They produce, farm, fatten and sell their own beef and lamb and also supply a full range of pork, chicken, duck, game and traditional handmade sausages. All sourced from local farms and estates within a 15 mile radius and prepared fresh daily for customers.

THREE LITTLE PIGS
Kiplingcotes Farm, Dalton Holme, Beverley, HU17 7PY.
www.threelittlepigschorizo.co.uk
Three Little Pigs is a perfectionist award-winning producer of cured meats based in Yorkshire, making hand finished chorizo and salami from rare breed pigs.

DAIRY

G G BAYNES & SON
Marley Cote Walls, Slaley, Hexham, NE47 0DQ.
T: 01434 673 244 www.marleycote.co.uk
Northumberland pedigree milk and cream.

DELIFRESH
59-62 St James's Market, Essex Street, Bradford,
West Yorkshire, BD4 7PG.
T: 01274 743737
Delifresh are passionate about fresh produce, dairy, cheese and speciality flavours. They deliver into kitchens throughout the north of the UK on a daily basis.

PARLOUR MADE ARTISAN CHEESE
Village Farm Dairy, Morden, Sedgefield, TS21 2EY.
T: 01740 622 255 www.parlourmade.co.uk

SHEPHERD'S PURSE
Leachfield Grange, Newsham, Thirsk,
North Yorkshire, YO7 4DJ.
T: 01845 587 220 www.shepherdspurse.co.uk
Shepherd's Purse is a small, family run, artisan cheese company producing the finest, traditional and continental style cheeses on their farm in North Yorkshire.

FINE & SPECIALITY FOODS

CQS CONTINENTAL QUATTRO STAGIONI
Unit 20/Eleventh Avenue, Gateshead, NE11 0JY.
T: 0191 487 3388
CQS is a specialist Italian food supplier and importer.

DELI FRESH
Kingsway North, Team Valley, Gateshead, NE1 1OS.
T: 0191 487 6177
Supplies bespoke regional fresh produce daily. If you ever need that little something different, they will source it for you.

MILLER FOOD SERVICE
David Miller Frozen Foods Ltd, 27 Hospital Fields Road,
York, YO10 4DZ.
T: 01904 655 368
Miller Food Service supply with all dry goods such as spices etc.

WELLOCKS
4 Pendleside, Nelson, Lancashire, BB9 6SH.
T: 08444 993 444 www.wellocks.co.uk
The key to Wynyard Hall Hotel's seasonally changing menus across all sites is the quality local ingredients and service provided by Wellocks food suppliers.

FRESH PRODUCE

KEN HOLLAND, PERFECT PRODUCE
The Old Barn, Vallum Farm, Newcastle, NE18 0LL.
T: 01434 672 323 www.vallumfarm.co.uk

TIM PYBUS, VILLAGE FARM
Main Street, West Tanfield, Ripon,
North Yorkshire, HG4 5JJ.
Supplier of delicious free-range eggs.

315
HINTS & TIPS...

HOW TO MAKE ICE CREAM WITHOUT A MACHINE

Although relatively inexpensive these days, not everyone has access to an ice cream machine. That's no reason not to follow some of these delicious recipes found in the Relish North East and Yorkshire book. Although more time consuming than a machine, excellent results can be obtained by following this simple method.

Follow the recipe right up until it tells you to churn in the machine, including any chilling time in the fridge.

Take your mixture from the fridge and stir with a rubber spatula. Transfer it to a suitable plastic container with a lid. There should be at least 2cm space at the top to allow the mixture to expand when freezing. Cover and place in the freezer for two hours.

Remove from the freezer and beat with a hand mixer, still in the container, to break up the ice crystals that are beginning to form. Cover and return to the freezer for a further 2 hours. (If you don't have a hand mixer then you may use a fork and some 'elbow grease' to break up the crystals).

Remove from the freezer and beat again with the hand mixer. The ice cream should be thickening up nicely at this point but too soft to scoop. Return it to the freezer for an additional hour. Beat again. If your ice cream is still not thickened sufficiently, repeat this process again after another hour. When the ice cream has thickened properly, stir in any add-ins at this point (honeycomb, nuts...). Do not beat with the hand mixer after the add-ins have been mixed in.

Place the tightly sealed container in the freezer and allow the ice cream to freeze until firm. The ice cream should be removed from the freezer 15-20 minutes before you wish to eat it. This will make scooping easier.

This method will also work for sorbets. Sometimes sorbets may go a bit 'icy' or 'crumbly' if left for too long in the freezer. This can be rectified by blitzing in a food processor just before serving.

Baked Dark Chocolate 'Millionaire'Pudding - **Page 216**

HOW TO MAKE A SUGAR STOCK SYRUP

This makes about 750ml sugar stock. It can be stored in a sterilised jar in the fridge for a couple of months.

500g white sugar
500ml water

Place the sugar and water in a pan. Dissolve slowly over a very low heat. You must not allow the syrup to boil until all the sugar has dissolved, about 5 minutes. Once completely dissolved, bring to the boil, then simmer for 5 minutes.

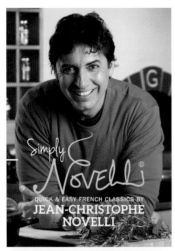

Simply
Novelli
QUICK & EASY FRENCH CLASSICS BY
JEAN-CHRISTOPHE
NOVELLI

Relish
COTSWOLDS &
OXFORDSHIRE

Original recipes from the Cotswolds and
Oxfordshire's finest chefs and restaurants.

OVER 100
RECIPES

Relish
NORTH EAST
& YORKSHIRE

Original recipes from the North East
and Yorkshire's finest chefs and
restaurants. Introduction by celebrity chefs
James Martin and Hairy Biker, Si King.

Relish
SOUTH WEST

Original recipes from the South West's
finest chefs and restaurants.
Introduction by Michael Caines MBE.

Relish
WALES
SECOND HELPING

Original recipes from the region's
finest chefs and restaurants.
Introduction by James Sommerin.

Relish
NORTH WEST

Original recipes from the region's
finest chefs and restaurants.
Introduction by Paul Heathcote, MBE.

Relish
SOUTH EAST

Original recipes from the region's
finest chefs and restaurants.
Introduction by Angela Hartnett, MBE.

Relish
SCOTLAND
THIRD HELPING

Original recipes from the region's finest chefs
and restaurants. Featuring the Michelin starred
chefs of Scotland.

Relish
MIDLANDS
SECOND HELPING

Original recipes from the region's finest chefs
and restaurants. Introduction by Adam Stokes.

HERE'S WHAT SOME OF BRITAIN'S BEST CHEFS HAVE SAID ABOUT WORKING WITH RELISH

"Relish books are full of enjoyable recipes and ideas for making the most edible treasures we have on our doorstep; both places to eat them and new, exciting ways to cook them."
Angela Hartnett, MBE

"The Relish cookbook offers the home cook some great inspiration to make the most of these wonderful ingredients in season." *Tom Kitchin, The Kitchin, Edinburgh*

"With mouth-watering, easy to follow recipes and beautiful photography, this book is a must have for any foodie, from professional chef to the inspired home cook."
Michael Caines MBE

Relish Midlands is a fantastic recipe book that brings together so many of the talented chefs and quality restaurants in the area. It gives you a taste of what our exciting region has to offer as well as the encouragement to try some new recipes. *Adam Stokes*

"Relish Wales Second Helping has been lovingly created and showcases the very best of our beautiful land. Great chefs, great food and sumptuous dishes. It makes for essential reading and I'm proud to be part of it." *James Sommerin*

"The Relish team has truly been amazing to work with. To have produced my book within two months from start to finish, only shows how professional a team of people can be."
Jean-Christophe Novelli

CALLING ALL CHEFS! ISN'T IT ABOUT TIME YOU FEATURED IN ONE OF OUR BOOKS?

Relish Publications is an independent publishing house based in North East England. The business was founded on an award-winning series of restaurant guides and recipe books featuring each region across England, Scotland and Wales. Relish has now worked with over 1,500 leading chefs and restaurants, building a portfolio of beautifully illustrated guides which are stocked nationally in Waterstones, Harvey Nichols, in each featured restaurant, in leading independent stores and online globally.

Relish has a small, friendly professional team, with experience in publishing, print management, editing, proofing, photography, design and artwork, sales distribution and marketing.

Relish Publications ensure a personal approach to every single customer, working exceptionally hard to develop a great product which reflects each chef's talent and passion.

Duncan and Teresa Peters established the company in 2009, with a vision of building a niche publishing house for food lovers. The success of Relish is now reflected in the fact that they have an ongoing programme of regional books, with many regions now having a Second and Third Helping (edition) of the leading restaurant guide and dozens of independent commissions from internationally celebrated chefs including Jean Christophe Novelli.

To find out how your chef or restaurant can be featured or discuss your publishing requirements simply log on to our publishing website www.relish-publishing.co.uk or call our head office on 01670 571 635 and speak to one of our team.

319
GLOSSARY

BAIN-MARIE
A pan or other container of hot water with a bowl placed on top of it. This allows the steam from the water to heat the bowl so ingredients can be gently heated or melted.

BLANCH
Boiling an ingredient before removing it and plunging it in ice cold water in order to stop the cooking process.

CARTOUCHE
A piece of greaseproof paper that covers the surface of a stew, soup, stock or sauce to reduce evaporation.

CHINOIS
A conical sieve with an extremely fine mesh. It is used to strain custards, purées, soups and sauces, producing a very smooth texture.

CLARIFIED BUTTER/CLARIFYING
Milk fat rendered from butter to separate the milk solids and water from the butter fat.

CONFIT
A method of cooking where the meat is cooked and submerged in a liquid to add flavour. Often this liquid is rendered fat. Confit can also apply to fruits - fruit confits are cooked and preserved in sugar, the result is like candied fruits.

EMULSION/EMULSIFY
In the culinary arts, an emulsion is a mixture of two liquids that would ordinarily not mix together, like oil and vinegar.

FRENCH TRIMMED
To French trim, fat, meat or skin is cut away to expose a piece of bone, so that it sticks out.

It also means that any excess fat is cut off. French Trimming can be done to lamb chops and bigger cuts; it can even can be done to chicken legs or breasts.

JULIENNE
A culinary knife cut in which the vegetable is sliced into long thin strips, similar to matchsticks.

MACERATE
Raw, dried, or preserved fruit and vegetables soaked in a liquid to soften the food or to absorb the flavour.

MIREPOIX
Finely diced combination of celery (pascal, celery or celeriac), onions and carrots. There are many regional mirepoix variations, which can sometimes be just one of these ingredients, or include additional spices creating a rich, flavoursome base to sauces or stews.

PANE
To coat with flour, beaten egg and breadcrumbs for deep frying.

PATE A BOMBE
A pâte à bombe is the French term for a mixture used as a base for making chocolate mousse and other mousse-like desserts.

PLANCHA
A type of flattop grill used for cooking, which is composed of a thick plate of metal above the heating element to provide thermal mass and eliminate hotspots.

QUENELLE
A neat, three-sided oval (resembling a mini rugby ball) that is formed by gently smoothing the mixture between two dessert spoons.

SABAYON
Made by beating egg yolks with a liquid over simmering water until thickened and increased in volume. The liquid can be water, but Champagne or wine is often used.

SOUS VIDE
French for 'under vacuum.' A method of cooking food sealed in airtight plastic bags in a water bath or in a temperature-controlled steam environment for longer than normal cooking times. The intention is to cook the item evenly, ensuring that the inside is properly cooked without overcooking the outside, and to retain moisture.

CONVERSION CHART

COOKING TEMPERATURES

Degrees Celsius	Fahrenheit	Gas Mark
140	275	1
150	300	2
160-170	325	3
180	350	4
190	375	5
200-210	400	6
220	425	7
230	450	8
240	475	9

*Temperatures for fan-assisted ovens are, as a general rule, normally about 20°C lower than regular oven temperature.

WEIGHT MEASUREMENT CONVERSIONS

1 teaspoon (5ml/5g)	$^1/_4$ oz
1 tablespoon (15ml/15g)	$^3/_4$ oz
10g	$^1/_2$ oz
25g	1oz
50g	2oz
75g	3oz
150g	5oz
200g	7oz
250g	9oz
350g	12oz
450g	1lb
1kg	2.2lb

VOLUME MEASUREMENT CONVERSIONS

55ml	2 fl oz
150ml	$^1/_4$ pt
275ml	$^1/_2$ pint
570ml	1 pt
1 litre	$1^3/_4$ pt